Illustrated

Fifties & Sixties Ford

BUYER'S GUIDE™

Illustrated

Fifties & Sixties Ford

BUYER'S GUIDE™

The golden days of Ford: 1946-1972
Fairlane to Mustang

PAUL R WOUDENBERG

Osceola, Wisconsin 54020, USA ®

First published in 1988 by Motorbooks International Publishers & Wholesalers Inc, PO Box 2, 729 Prospect Avenue, Osceola, WI 54020 USA

Printed and bound in the United States of America

Library of Congress Cataloging-in-Publication Data
Woudenberg, Paul R.
Illustrated fifties and sixties Ford buyer's guide.

1. Ford automobile—Purchasing. I. Title.
TL215.F7W683 1988 629.2'222 87-24799
ISBN 0-87938-278-3 (pbk.)

On the cover: The quintessential Ford of the fifties and sixties, the Fairlane Crown Victoria, photographed by Jerry Heasley.

Motorbooks International books are also available at discounts in bulk quantity for industrial or sales-promotional use. For details write to Special Sales Manager at the Publisher's address

Contents

Acknowledgments

The Ford Motor Company has graciously and generously supported this project. In particular, all photographs, unless otherwise credited, are from Ford. Thanks are due also to Don Petersen, chairman of the board; David Scott, vice-president of Public Affairs; Roland W. Williams, corporate projects manager, Public Affairs; and Bill Buffa, researcher in the Photo Media department.

The Ford fraternity is an unusually knowledgeable group of enthusiasts, and I have sought the help of experts in many fields. Bill Barber and Bill Logan of the Galaxie Club reviewed the Galaxie chapter. Tom Howard gave useful advice and help on cars of the fifties and early sixties. Ted Davidson reviewed the material on the four-seater Thunderbirds. Mitch Reed gave many helpful suggestions and proofed the text on the early T-Birds. John Gunnell, editor of that most useful journal, *Old Cars Weekly*, provided the auction information.

I especially wish to acknowledge the great help of Gary and Linda Richards. Gary, former president of the Fabulous Fifties Ford Club of America, compiled the material on engines and drivelines. In addition, he proofed the manuscript and gave me the benefit of his vast knowledge and rich archives.

Barbara Harold's superb editorial eye saves writers from numerous blunders and I am indebted to her.

Finally, I wish to thank my daughter, Betsy, who corrected the manuscript, proving once again that the pen is mightier than the word.

Though the help of so many Ford friends has been an important factor in assuring the accuracy of this text, errors no doubt remain which are, of course, my responsibility. Criticisms and suggestions are very welcome.

Paul R. Woudenberg, Ph.D.
Pebble Beach, California
August 1987

Introduction

Post-1945 Fords offer the greatest variety of rewards for collectors, enthusiasts and investors for many reasons.

1. The Ford market is the largest in the world. One quarter of the advertising in *Hemmings Motor News* for automotive sales, literature, parts and service is about Fords.

2. Ford parts and restoration service are everywhere. Sheet metal is available for virtually all cars; mechanical parts are easy to find and even body hardware is usually available. When it comes to parts, no car is easier to restore.

3. The Ford is a tough and reliable runner. Many collectible Fords are still in daily service simply because they can be driven, maintained and repaired more cheaply than a new car.

4. The collectible Ford is a very practical car to own; it will not "eat you alive" in upkeep. It can be shown, rallied, enjoyed and yet driven to work daily. It is fun to drive.

5. The Ford offers many different body styles and models that can satisfy the tastes of almost all collectors. Ford was a leading builder of convertibles and station wagons. The Thunderbird, Mustang and the great muscle cars targeted special markets with huge success. The specialty cars such as the retractable hardtops, the Sportsmans and the Starliners offer a buyer scope for particular interests.

6. Fords come in all price ranges. Some postwar Fords such as the F-type blown Thunderbird are exceeding $50,000 in price. Yet for $5,000 you can buy a very usable convertible from the sixties. Entry-level Ford collectibles with standard closed bodies can sometimes be bought for as little as $500.

7. There are more than twenty-two clubs for post-1945 Fords. No matter what sort of Ford you choose, there will be a club to supply you with a journal, membership lists and help. Clubs also mean rallies, shows and friends to help you get going in the hobby. Ford club members are some of the most friendly folks anywhere. They are eager to welcome new members and go out of their way to make Ford ownership a pleasure.

8. The prices of Fords are rising. As this Buyer's Guide will show, certain Ford models are appreciating tremendously. Even the most garden-variety Ford is slowly gaining value. There are many reasons for this, not the least of which is that the older Ford car (the A, T and early V-8) led the way as a collectible some thirty years ago. The post-1945 Ford continued this leadership as new and younger hobbyists entered the field. Fords are the premier entry car for new collectors, and this has led to price leadership throughout the years.

The rating system

The five star system, pioneered by Dean Batchelor and used by me in previous works, has been modified as follows for use in this Buyer's Guide.

★ Models in abundant supply which have slow upward appreciation. Prices may be very low, though fine examples may command higher prices if for no other reason than they provide good transportation. These cars offer a good and inexpensive entry access to the hobby.

★★ Models that have found substantial collector interest and are being bought and held for future appreciation. Unrestored examples may still be bargains, though restorers are investing in rebuilds with confidence in their future value.

★★★ Models that have had greater appreciation and are targeted by collectors. Bargains are rarely available in this group. Most convertibles in all models will have *at least* this rating

★★★★ Models that have had long-term recognized collector interest and accompanying appreciation.

★★★★★ Particular models of exceptional interest and rarity which have realized their highest values and have strongest collector interest.

Auction prices

Within each chapter are representative recent auction prices drawn from *Old Cars Weekly*. The rating system follows that of *Old Cars Weekly*, which is in general use. However, for the purposes of this book, cars are considered *only* in condition 1 or 2 (noted in parentheses) which are defined as follows:

Condition 1: Excellent; restored to current maximum professional standards of quality in every area, or perfect original with all components operating like new. A 95-plus show car that is not driven.

Condition 2: Fine; well restored, or a combination of superior restoration and excellent original; or an extremely well maintained original showing very minimal wear.

Keep in mind that condition 3 is Very Good, 4 is Good and 5 is Restorable. Most cars are found in condition 3 (presentable and serviceable) or lower, hence the prices quoted will be on the high side of the market.

All prices are *highest* in a specific category, year and condition unless followed by an L, which indicates *lowest* price. Keep in mind also that auction markets vary widely. A small regional auction may show lower prices, while famous national auctions such as the January Scottsdale/Phoenix season may bring uniquely high prices. For regular and detailed reporting on auction prices, consult *Old Cars Weekly*.

Chapter 1

1946-1948

★★★	
★★★★	Convertible
★★★★★	Sportsman

History

The first nonproduction handmade 1946 Ford was shown on June 2, 1945, the earliest postwar announcement in the industry. Production was under way by October 26 and picked up slowly because of strikes and shortages. The 1946 was, in essence, the 1942 model with minor styling changes. The rather fussy 1942 grille was discarded in favor of a bolder pattern featuring three horizontal bars with a strong capping bar. The design was broken up by indented, red painted grooves. Two horizontal trim strips were mounted at the rear deck-lid handle.

The 1942 Ford had a brief life but was reincarnated in the first postwar prototype on June 2, 1945, with very few changes. The 1946 factory list prices for new cars were actually lower than the Office of Price Adminstration maximum used-car prices for the 1942 model.

The 221 ci V-8 engine of 1942 was dropped in favor of the 239 ci engine used in the 1942 Mercury, which was rated at 100 bhp. It then became the standard V-8 engine for both Ford and Mercury production. The greater weight of the Mercury meant that the Ford was the faster car, a shift from prewar images.

Prices were set initially by the Office of Price Administration at about nine percent above 1942 levels, which caused Ford to lose $300 per car in 1945. Only 34,439 units were built in that year, and the situation was intolerable. Two price increases were granted in the spring of 1946. By then, the least expensive Ford, the three-passenger coupe, listed for nearly the price of the 1942 V-8 convertible coupe.

The 1947 Ford was introduced in January 1947; the 1948 model began production the following November and ended in May 1948. Production figures accurately reflect these varying time spans, since the company was producing to maximum volume throughout the period.

Identification

1946: Grille with red trim, parking lights set above the grille, two trim strips on trunk. "Super Deluxe" in script below left headlamp, instruments with red numerals on black background on Super Deluxe with gray backgrounds, Deluxe instrument panel in brown tones.

The 1946 postwar Ford was in production on October 26, 1945. The bold horizontal bars of the grille plus minor trim changes added strength to the design. This Deluxe Tudor sedan had an initial F.O.B. price of $979, and Ford claimed that it lost $300 on every car. By late 1946 the F.O.B. price of the Deluxe Tudor had risen to $1,179.

1947: Earliest trim was identical to 1946 but in January, plain chrome bars and round parking lights were introduced. The hood was also plain without ornament. The instruments were in gold tones on mottled backgrounds. About May, a new hood ornament appeared.

1948: Similar to 1947, except ignition steering-wheel lock, a feature of Fords since 1932, was omitted in favor of a rotary key lock mounted in the same location by the steering column.

Serial numbers (engine numbers, including truck production):

1946: Six-cylinder, 1GA 227524 to 326417.
Eight-cylinder, 99A 650280 to 1412707.

1947: Six-cylinder, 71GA 326418 to 414366, 77HA 0512 to 9038.
Eight-cylinder, 799A 1412708 to 2071231.

1948: Six-cylinder, 87HA 0536 to 73901.
Eight-cylinder, 899A 1984589 to 2381447.

(Keep in mind that early 1947 production model may outwardly resemble the 1946 model.)

Body styles

The Deluxe model was offered in Fordor, Tudor and coupe styles with both six- and eight-cylinder engines; these models have the lowest collectible value. (The quaint spellings of two- and four-doors continued

It was a lucky buyer who was able to find one of these handsome 1946 club coupes or sedan coupes as Ford called them. Though 70,826 were built in that first postwar year, demand was exceptional. Only in the spring of 1949 did used-car values for this model fall below the new list price in 1946 of $1,223. The sedan coupe remains a desirable collectible.

until 1963.) In the Super Deluxe lines, two additional bodies were added to the original three: the sedan coupe (or club coupe) and the station wagon. The V-8 Super Deluxe alone offered the convertible.

The one new model was the Sportsman convertible, a wood-paneled steel-framed body using station wagon styling. It was a rarity even in 1946 when only 723 were sold. At 3,366 pounds, it was 100 pounds heavier than the standard convertible. Publicity included a set of four of the new models made available to Jack Benny's Sportsmen Quartet. Production peaked in 1947 with 2,774 examples, while only twenty-eight of the 1948 model were built.

Regular convertible production was 16,359 cars for 1946, 22,159 for 1947 and 12,033 for 1948. Station wagon production was 16,960 units for 1946, 16,104 for 1947 and 8,912 for 1948. Such substantial production makes these sought-after models still available. Today, a rarer model would be the five-window business coupe, which never achieved much volume after 1946. Only 10,872 coupes were sold in 1947 and 5,048 in 1948. Most have perished but, despite rarity, collectors have not driven prices upward, the fate of so many closed cars.

Problem areas

This historic overheating problem of the early V-8s, caused by the exhaust porting passing across the block, continued in this series. The twenty-two-quart radiator was huge but overheating could still occur. The

The Sportsman convertible premiered in the late spring of 1946. The novel wooden trim was striking but added 100 pounds to the convertible's weight. The original F.O.B. price was $1,865, about that of a 1946 Cadillac 61 coupe. Demand was strong for the meager 723 units available in 1946, and used-car value a year later was around $2,600. Notice the power windows. These cars can bring over $30,000 today.

top-mounted fuel pump in the cradle of the V-8 engine was subject to vapor lock under hot conditions.

In all other respects, the 1946-48 series was a very tough car, the last expression of the original Ford chassis layout dating back to the Model T. The transverse springs were still there, tamed with stabilizer bars and a transverse link. The differential with straddle-mounted pinions dated from 1935. The synchromesh box was the 1939 ball-retainer blocker-type design with the 1940 side-shifting links. The engine was based on the 1939 revision of the original 1932 unit. Every part of the car benefited from fifteen years of refinement of a stable design.

The touch-bar tuning radio was a clumsy device even when new, but was a solid unit and responds to rebuilds. Plastic instrument panel parts that have decayed are remanufactured by private vendors from time to time.

A strong frame and traditional body assembly methods have made the 1946-48 series relatively resistant to rust when compared to later designs. Removable fenders make repair and replacement easy. Survivors by now have received decent care, and the chance of finding a solid car is good. Nevertheless, a careful check of lower body panels and lower trunk area is essential.

Summary and prospects

These early postwar Fords give great driving pleasure and remain the last of the "pony" cars produced by the company. They are prewar cars, technically and stylistically, and thus benefit from the enthusiasm shown for Fords of the thirties.

The market for the various closed bodies is about the same, and for first-class cars hovers in the $6,000 to $8,000 range. Six-cylinder cars will bring a bit less; the club coupe will be worth a bit more. Bargains are not common in this market because, though the survival rate of these cars has been good, by now most have found their way into

The early 1947 Deluxe Tudor simplified the 1946 trim. The hood ornament, missing in this early-production photo, was added in late spring. The Tudor was the most popular body style, and 180,649 were sold in 1947 in Deluxe and Super Deluxe forms. But for collectors, they represent the least-desirable model.

appreciative hands. Beware of cars that have suffered from old customizing jobs or "hotting up," which usually reduces value. There is, however, an esoteric market for specialized customs which can bring high prices.

The station wagon will bring much more, with prices in the $15,000 to $20,000 range, for cars in top condition. Restoration costs are higher for wooden bodies, so check carefully for wet and dry rot. Bad examples could be for sale very cheap.

The convertible coupe is much sought after, and top prices are at $20,000, though good examples may be found in the $15,000 range. The Sportsman convertible can bring up to $35,000 at a top auction for pristine examples, though, like the station wagons, less-than-perfect examples may be much less expensive. The Sportsman represents the very top of Ford pricing for early postwar V-8s.

The future appreciation of the 1946-48 seems to be slow and steady. Younger collectors are often drawn to the cars of the fifties and sixties, leaving the early postwar cars to older buyers. The thought of paying $20,000 for a 1946 Ford convertible may shock those with long memories, but Ford buyers seem legion and it is a huge market. Market values were depressed in the early 1980s but have now recovered.

For a long-range investment that can bring much reliable driving pleasure, these lovely old cars have few equals.

Production:
1946 467,536
1947 430,198
1948 247,724

Auction prices

1946 convertible (1)	$24,000
1946 convertible (2)	$17,500
1946 Tudor (2)	$6,500
1947 convertible (2)	$14,500
1948 convertible (2)	$14,500

This 1947 Ford convertible was a strong seller when new and continues to draw collector interest today. Prices for superb examples have now passed $20,000.

The instrument panels of the 1947 and 1948 models were identical except for the ignition switch. Shown here is the conventional rotary key at the steering column of the 1948 model, which replaced the traditional Ford steering lock introduced in 1932.

The Fordor Deluxe sedan was another popular car, and this 1948 model shows the hood ornament that was added in mid-1947. The model has been skillfully posed in front of the rear door to deemphasize the protruding hinge in front of the rear quarter window. There are not many of these Fordors left, though prices are about the same as the Tudors.

This 1948 station wagon (externally the same as the 1947), is a sought-after collectible. It was expensive in 1948, with an F.O.B. price of $1,972. In 1955 this wagon could be bought for about $250. This is the reason many were junked as the bodies decayed. The few survivors in restored condition can bring upwards of $20,000 or even more.

Chapter 2

1949-1951

★★	
★★★	Special bodies

History

In April 1946, Ernest Breech, soon to be the executive vice-president and chief operating officer at Ford, took a look at the proposed 1949 Ford created by E.T. Gregorie, longtime Ford designer. It was a big car, and

This multi-highlighted front view of the then-new 1949 Ford was taken in the spring of 1948 and dramatizes the total break with previous styling. The car caused a sensation when introduced on June 8, 1948. Prices were edging up; this custom Tudor had an F.O.B. price of $1,590.

on September 3 this prototype was designated by Breech as the 1949 Mercury. The absence of a Ford prototype was then crucial, and a crash program resulted. Gregorie and an outside designer, George Walker, both prepared new proposals. On December 11, the design by Walker was chosen over that of Gregorie, who resigned four days later. Walker soon took over Ford styling.

The 1949 car was exceptionally clean with slab sides and clear angular window openings. Glass area was tremendously increased; the rear window was eighty-eight percent larger. If the bumpers hung out a bit, at least they were without ornamentation. The grille owed something to the 1947 Studebaker, with a circular bull's-eye dead center on which a "6" or "8" announced engine specification. The dash layout was entirely new, with "black light" illuminating a large circular instrument layout directly in front of the driver. Interior room was greatly increased, and consequently passengers remembered no relationship to past Ford practices and proportions.

The chassis was a total break with Ford tradition and featured Hotchkiss drive with hypoid rear axle, independent front Hydra-coil suspension and half-elliptic Para-Flex rear springs. The ride was on par with the best of the competition.

The engine was refined, though still with the basic V-8 and six-cylinder layouts. A conventional ignition tower was fitted to the V-8. To those Ford fans who were shocked by all the changes, the familiar starter whine was reassuring. Overdrive was available which, when used with a 4.1:1 rear axle ratio, produced 65 mph at 2306 rpm. Normal rear axle ratio was 3.73:1.

The car was announced on June 8, 1948, and received a very enthusiastic reception by

The 1949 convertible continued Ford's dominance of the open-car market with this handsome car. Ford sold a tremendous 51,133 units. New 1949 convertibles listed for well over $2,000 in 1948 and 1949. Today, prices for the finest examples are in five figures and move upward from $15,000.

dealers and the public. The new Ford sold at a substantial premium over list price. The November 1948 *Kelley Blue Book* showed early used prices $1,000 over factory list which, when applied to the least expensive coupe, amounted to a fifty percent premium! The market stabilized quickly in early 1949, but even in January 1950 used prices for 1949s were virtually the same as new factory-list prices some eighteen months earlier.

The 1950 model, on sale in November 1949, offered minor refinements and trim changes, the most obvious being the new push-button door handles.

For 1951, the new Fordomatic was offered, essentially a planetary transmission with a two-speed Drive range plus a Low range. Low gear was not used in normal driving unless manually selected; standing starts in Drive range were in second gear. Acceleration was not all that brisk, a fact acknowledged by the factory when it specified that a vacuum booster windshield wiper was fitted to all automatic and overdrive cars on the assumption that the throttle would often be well-opened.

The 1951 model abandoned the single bull's-eye grille in place of two bull's-eyes set behind the bumper guards. The instruments remained in a single central circle, but the speedometer needle was tipped with a lighted circle which illuminated the speedometer numbers. The dash was redesigned featuring an asymmetrical metallic inset panel on the driver's side, with the various controls softly lighted. The interior of the 1951 was much improved in both design and finish materials.

Identification

1949: Central bull's-eye in grille with parking lights at tips of middle bar. Block-letter "FORD" above grille. Pull-out door handles.

1950: Parking lights moved below center bar. Medallion replaces "FORD" above grille. Push-button door handles.

1951: Two bull's-eyes in grille. New instrument panel with a satin chrome perforated background. Safety Glow illumination behind each control knob on dash. New control panel for heater with sliding controls.

The 1950 grille center bar was extended to the edge of the body emphasizing width and massiveness. The replacement of the block "Ford" letters on the front of the hood with a medallion helped to simplify and strengthen the appearance. Sales in 1950 were record-breaking for this very popular model. Prices today for restored examples of this superb convertible are approaching $20,000.

The 1949 instrument panel was fresh and clean. The speedometer had black light and was much easier to read. The MagicAire heater box was hung on the firewall—no integration of the heater system in sight, yet. The greater width of the interior is dramatically apparent.

The Crestliner was introduced in midseason and perhaps bore some resemblance to the customized Fords on California streets. Its humble Tudor origins were still evident and sales were modest. The hardtop Victoria of 1951, in essence, finished the Crestliner. Good clean Crestliners today are strong collectibles. In 1951, Victorias outsold the increasingly rare Crestliners 12 to 1, which may account for price parity today (around $8,000 for top cars).

Serial numbers:
1949 (start June 1948):
Six-cylinder, 98HA 101 to 173310.
Eight-cylinder, 98BA 101 to 948236.
1950 (start November 1949):
Six-cylinder, HO followed by assembly plant code (i.e., HOAT).
Eight-cylinder, BO followed by assembly plant code (i.e., BOBF).
1951 (start November 1950):
Six-cylinder, H1 followed by assembly plant code.
Eight-cylinder, B1 followed by assembly plant code.

A special police engine with 255.4 ci displacement was available and engine numbers beginning with P reflect this.

The assembly plant codes are as follows: Atlanta, AT; Buffalo, BF; Chester, CS; Chicago, CH; Dallas, DL; Dearborn, DR; Edgewater, EG; Kansas City, KC; Long Beach, LB; Louisville, LU; Memphis, MP; Norfolk, NR; Richmond, RH; Somerville, SR; St. Paul, SP; Highland Park, HM.

Body styles

The station wagons were built with steel framing. For 1949 and early 1950, wooden panels and trim were mounted on the frame. Later wagons used metal panels with applied simulated woodgraining, a metal tailgate and wood trim. All wagons had only two heavy doors. Both the second and third seats were removable for cargo loading. In late 1950, the middle seat folded flat. The "Country Squire" name was first used in the 1950 model year. Tires on the wagons were 7.10x15.

The Crestliner appeared in 1950, essentially a two-door with vinyl top, special side-paint combinations, more chrome, different wheel covers and a special steering wheel.

A more enduring style was the new Victoria in 1951, a pillarless Tudor. It was priced just $24 below the convertible coupe. Chrysler and General Motors had offered hardtop coupes in 1950. The Chrysler Town and Country series even had a low-production hardtop coupe in 1948. Ford's Victoria

The 1950 station wagon was in transition. This custom model still carried genuine wooden panels but soon had steel panels with simulated wood appliques. Restored wagons from 1949 to 1951 bring an easy five figures and are eagerly sought by collectors.

was an instant hit with over 110,286 units sold the first year, despite a late introduction. The Crestliner, however, had peaked at 17,601 units in 1950, and production fell in 1951 to only 8,703.

It is useful to keep in mind that the coupe, available all three years, was a short "greenhouse" Tudor, and in the deluxe line was a three-passenger business model. It is more highly regarded than the Tudor by collectors because the proportions may be better and the car itself is much rarer.

Convertible production was way up from the 1946-48 model. In 1949 it reached 51,133 (an eighteen-month production span). In 1951, convertible production was 40,934. Chevrolet had rivaled Ford's convertible production in the postwar years, but Ford easily dominated sales. Chevrolet offered a convertible again in 1950, but Ford easily dominated sales in 1950 and 1951.

Problem areas

The 1949 Ford had numerous teething troubles, as would be expected from a totally new car brought to production in less than two years. The chassis seemed more flexible than the traditional 1948, despite claims that the body structure was fifty-eight percent more rigid. In truth, the ride was more flexible and the car seemed to wallow when compared to the older, stiff transverse spring system. The wheelbase was longer and the car was lighter. The perception of flexibility was reinforced by squeaks and groans in the body. The pull-type door latches were particularly aggravating and door rattle was common. The car lacked the solid feeling of the older cars.

Almost all problems were corrected in the 1950 model, and thereafter the Ford recaptured its reputation for tough reliability. The new radiator system with Equa-Flo

This very simple 1951 Deluxe business coupe was the bottom of the line and cost $1,411 F.O.B. Though 6.00x16 tires were specified for the Deluxe line, this car has 6.70x15 tires. Only 20,343 were built, which may account for the fact that this body style will be worth a bit more than the ubiquitous Tudor sedan.

cooling was a substantial improvement. The duo-servo brakes with 173 square inches of lining area were self-energizing and needed lighter pedal pressure than the 1946-48 system, but were subject to grabbing.

Summary and prospects

The first truly postwar Fords, long neglected, have found a growing following among collectors, and prices have been steadily rising. Excellent examples of the closed cars may be found in the $6,000 to $7,000 range, with the club coupes leading the market. Many of these cars are marvelously original, discovered by collectors from longtime owners. Though there are still sedans available for very low prices, restoration costs are substantial and full restorations are justified economically only by the more desirable body types.

As an example, station wagons are readily bringing five-figure prices, and convertibles can reach $15,000 or even more. These figures provide room for substantial restoration investment, and both models should be rated three stars.

Within the three-year production span, the 1949s trail the other two model years in value, perhaps an echo of the original problems with the newly introduced model.

The Crestliner will bring a fifty percent premium because of low production and also should be rated three stars. The 1951 Victoria should do as well, if not better, even though production was very much higher. The six-cylinder cars always have lower value than the V-8s.

Be on the lookout for the early four-spoke X-type white steering wheel which was offered as an accessory when the 1949 model was introduced. A similar wheel in black was used on the later Crestliners. Original radios will add value but may also be found at swap meets and specialty dealers.

Production:

*1949** 1,118,762
1950 1,209,549
1951 1,013,381
**Eighteen months*

Auction prices

1949 Tudor coupe (2)	$6,500
1950 convertible (2)	$10,250
1950 business coupe (2)	$4,050
1950 Crestliner (2)	$7,100
1951 Victoria (2)	$4,100
1951 convertible (2)	$18,500

By 1951, the front end of the Ford was a more integrated design. The twin bull's-eyes and general redesign added to the grille mass. The 15 inch wheels made the car appear bigger. On the custom series, the side chrome strip extended around the back of the car. The 1950 and 1951 convertibles are at the top of collectibles in this series, with prices approaching $20,000 for the superb specimens.

Chapter 3

1952-1954

★
★★★ **Skyliners and Sunliners**

History

George Walker headed the styling of the 1952 Ford product line and, for the first time, the Ford, Mercury and Lincoln all had a strong family resemblance. The Ford was angular, neat and trim. The dashboard had a new integrated Flight Style instrument panel not unlike the Cadillac of 1948. Brake and clutch pedals were suspended. Curved windshields without the central dividing pillar added interior space.

Three model lines were offered: Mainline, Customline and Crestline. The new Tudor Mainline ranch wagon with metal side pan-

This tranquil family scene of middle America was the target market for the 1952 Ford Customline. George Walker's completely new styling was evident. In 1952, 188,303 buyers lined up for the Fordor, the largest-selling body type. Good 1952s are still very reasonable, but there are not many left of this low-production year.

els was a handsome response to the successful 1949 Plymouth Suburban. In the midrange Customline a similar but Fordor wagon was called the Country Sedan. The Crestline station wagon, now the Country Squire, offered wood trim attached to the Country Sedan, plus upgraded appointments. The pillarless Victoria coupe was continued in the Crestline series as was the Sunliner convertible.

In 1954, the Crestline Victoria was offered with a clear plastic insert roof panel and was called the Skyliner. A four-door sedan was added to the Crestliner series with appropriate trim. A transparent lid was also used on the speedometer.

The 1952 dashboard was very neat. The big, central cowled instrument panel was a theme used in the 1948 Cadillac. Trim quality was improving. However, since it is hard to restore interiors, originality is crucial.

The 1954 model had many mechanical improvements, including ball-joint front suspension, power windows, power steering, power brakes and power seats. In particular, the new Y-block ohv V-8 engine was the first major redesign of the V-8 engine since 1939. Collectors have sought the "loaded" 1954 Crestline series, which, with the new ohv engine makes these cars seem more like the 1955 models than the 1953 model.

Identification

1952: Circular parking lights under the headlights. The central grille bar has a cutout, and in the center is a bull's-eye somewhat like the 1949 grille.

1953: Grille was simplified and the central bull's-eye became more of a bullet; in retrospect certainly the cleanest design of the three-year model run.

1954: Stylists returned to 1952 themes, again with a cutout on the central bar and small circular parking lights. Crestliner trim was a single bright spear extending the full length of the car at midbody line. The ohv V-8 engine is instantly identified by its valve covers.

The patent plate, found on the left-front body pillar, is a useful check.

The first letter of the serial number indicates engine according to the following code:
1952-53: B, 239 ci V-8, L-head, 110 bhp.
1952-54: A, 223 ci 6-cyl, ohv, 115 bhp.
1954: U, 239 ci V-8, ohv, 130 bhp.
1954: P, 256 ci V-8, ohv, 161 bhp (police).
The second figure, a numeral, indicates production year (2=1952, 3=1953 and so on); the third identifies assembly plant; and the fourth represents body type. For example: B3FX=a 110 hp V-8 (B), 1953 (3), made in Dearborn (F), with a Country Sedan body (X).

Utility and performance

The new Y-block engine in 1954 upped brake horsepower to 130, with substantial performance improvement. Chevrolet's V-8 did not appear until 1955, thus the horsepower race had not yet begun. Ford was the performance champion, a role it pursued vigorously.

The 1952-54 is a very useful car, somewhat slow by later standards yet simple to operate. The absence of power-assisted devices in 1952 and 1953 makes these cars easier to work on and restore. The ball-joint suspension in 1954, plus numerous power options such as steering, windows, brakes and seats, makes this model much more like the later cars.

Problem areas

As is the case with all automotive designs, long-term production brings heightened quality. By 1951, the chassis and driveline of the 1949 series had been perfected and the technology was carried over into the 1952 line. These cars have proven to be very reliable.

However, 6 volt electrics continued, which may prove anemic when starting. The heating problems of the L-head engine had diminished, although the cooling system must be kept clean. The Y-block engine solved the overheating problem.

The usual checks for rust in both body panels and suspension parts are advisable.

Summary and prospects

The 1952-54 cars were trendsetters for Ford and bear a resemblance to the later cars of the fifties. Paradoxically, their progressive styling is the reason they have been overlooked by collectors who, seeking an older style, are better satisfied by the 1949-51 series. Today's prices of the 1952s and 1953s are the lowest of any models of the decade.

The Mainline series are the plain-Janes of 1952-53 and have been sacrificed in the restoration of more glamorous bodies. The 1952 Victoria had a three-piece rear window and, next to the convertible Sunliner, has found favor with collectors. A superb 1952 Sunliner can bring $12,000 or more, while a first-class Crestline Victoria could bring $8,000. The Country Squire would be close behind the Victoria. The 1953 models should do fractionally better, but condition is all-important.

The other closed body styles have low

In 1953, sales doubled for Ford products. Styling revisions were minor; the central horizontal bar was stronger and a trim stripe appeared on the rear fender panel. This Customline Fordor was immensely popular in 1953. Collectors today prefer the Crestline series, but a superb Customline sedan can bring upwards of $5,000.

value, with top examples in the $4,000 to $5,000 range. Usually, however, good sedans can easily be found in the $2,000 range. Despite low prices, these cars are tough and reliable and will give much pleasure. They could be a fine bargain when entering the hobby.

The 1954 cars, so much like the 1953s yet with so many improvements, have greater value. The Skyliner Victoria is particularly popular and top examples can bring $10,000 or more. Sunliners are approaching the $13,000 range. Both of these models should be rated three stars, and much higher prices are likely in the near future.

The 1952-54 series, in general, has been appreciating at the rate of about five percent per year and should continue.

Production:
1952 671,733
1953 1,247,542
1954 1,165,942

Production (convertible):
1952 22,534
1953 40,861
1954 36,685

Auction prices
1953 Crestline convertible (2) $9,600
1954 Crestline covertible (2) $10,600

This 1953 Tudor Mainline sedan had the lowest collectibility for the 1950s. The absence of trim and the 6.00x16 tires add to its utilitarian look. Few of these cars have survived; some were sacrificed in the restoration of more desirable models.

The most valuable 1953 Ford is the Crestline Sunliner convertible, a very handsome car. Good examples command five figures. The simple wheel hubcaps were usually upgraded to the deluxe wheel covers.

The 1953 Crestline Country Squire was the top-of-the-line wagon and continued Ford's leadership in this popular style. It was the most expensive body style for 1953, and remains a fine collectible because of its rarity and distinctive appearance. Prices will reflect condition of the wood trim and interior, both costly to restore. Top examples may bring $7,000.

The 1954 Crestline Skyliner with the plastic roof panel is a superb collectible, and beautiful examples may bring five figures. Only 13,344 were built. This prototype retained the 1953 V-8 emblem on the front fender; the production emblem emphasized the new Y-block engine. Canadian-built flathead V-8s stayed with the 1953 emblem.

The Crestline Victoria was a very popular car and 95,464 were sold. Many are well preserved and loved, and with the new Y-block engine are very usable. Collectors have long favored this model.

The Mainline ranch wagon was introduced in 1952 and was a splendid utility vehicle. Collectors have not sought this car in part because it had the lowest trim level. However, it is still more desirable than the comparable closed sedans. Good examples are very reasonable.

This 1954 Crestline Fordor was highly trimmed and very sharp. The picture is of an early prototype which still carried 1953 wheel covers and V-8 emblem. A fine example of this car would bring $4,000 or more.

Chapter 4

1955-1956

History

The 1955 was substantially restyled as Ford prepared to face the new Chevrolet for a mighty year of competition. Horsepower was beginning to be a factor and the 239 ci Y-block was bored out to 272 ci. Brake horsepower went up from 130 to 162 and, following a compression hike in 1956, to 173. In 1955, both the Thunderbird and the Corvette offered high-performance engines which soon became optional in standard production.

The Fordomatic transmission provided a first-gear start under heavy throttle. This reliable Borg-Warner unit was used by Studebaker, Rambler, Jaguar, Checker and others, and previously offered only an automatic second-third shift with a manual first.

The splendid 1955 Fairlane Crown Victoria was instantly identified by the striking roll bar trim. This particular car lacks the Fordomatic or overdrive emblem on the deck and therefore must have had only the standard transmission. These Crown Victorias command high prices, with good examples easily surpassing $10,000. Collectors especially seek the rare Crown Victoria with transparent top, of which only 1,999 were built. These may bring $15,000 and up.

Factory air-conditioning was available in 1955 and is rare. The system suffered from ineffective ducting and clutching problems. It was not until 1959 that truly perfected air-conditioning arrived.

Twelve-volt electrics began in 1956, a welcome improvement.

The new top-of-the-line model replaced the Crestline and was called the Fairlane (after Henry Ford, Sr.'s Dearborn home). All Fairlanes and station wagons had dual-exhaust systems. A safety emphasis in 1956 produced recessed steering wheels and padded dashes.

The Crown Victorias, with their distinctive strong central chrome pillar which passed over the top of the car, were offered in 1955 and 1956.

Identification

Serial identification of all Ford engines including the Y-block may be found in the Appendix. The claim of a high-performance Thunderbird engine (P) in a standard car may thus be easily checked.

The 1955 Mainline dash with standard features. There was no horn ring, and both the steering wheel and control knobs were black. The rubber mat was expected in the Mainline and Customline models. Even the Fairlane hardtop with vinyl seats had rubber mats, but with cloth interior the Fairlanes came with carpeting. The radio was basic, as was the heater which did not have any fresh-air ducting.

The Fairlane town sedan was the top-of-the-line four-door and was the biggest seller of any 1955 body style with 224,872 units. This popularity when new has not continued into the collector market where Victorias are preferred. Prices for best town sedans range from $5,000 to $6,000.

The most important visual clue is the vertical A-pillar at the front door, which required the pronounced wraparound windshield. Strong rear fins dominated the rear view of the car. The front grille had a screen with square holes concealing the dark open recesses which had characterized the 1949-54 models. These little squares became rectangles in 1956; the stylists played with these screen designs in each successive model year.

The Fairlane introduced a new slash stripe on the side of the car, sharply dipping to a point in the middle of the front door. It was a dramatic and often bizarre touch, symbolic of the fifties. The stylists continued to work themes on side panels, but avoided some of the excesses of General Motors and Chrysler which climaxed in the 1959 cars.

Utility and performance

Engine horsepower was increasing rapidly. In just three years, the modest 110 bhp of the final flathead V-8 in 1953 had reached a maximum of 198 bhp in the T-Bird Y-block 292 ci 4V engine. Performance was transformed and by 1956 was up to present-day standards.

Problem areas

The buyer of a fifties Ford may often confront a stored car with a Fordomatic transmission that has been idle. On a test-drive, check for slipping which will indicate damage and the need for a rebuild. Slow engagement when cold indicates hard seals. Leaking when cold is not uncommon; as seals expand, the leaking stops. Look under car after a cold start for leaks.

With modern oil, the life of a Fordomatic is 100,000 miles, but in the fifties models, transmission rebuilds might be needed at 60,000 miles. Type A automatic transmission fluid could cause varnish. Type F was an improved fluid and was used through the sixties. Modern fluids such as Dexron 2 have further extended transmission life. However, there are cars that have never had the

The 1955 Fairlane Sunliner convertible coupe was ever popular and retains top value in today's market. Even fair examples will rarely be seen under $10,000, while fine specimens will readily make $20,000. This is an early model, with the two-piece molding over the windshield. One-piece moldings began in midyear of production.

transmission fluid touched, thus a careful check will be prudent.

If the car has manual steering, a shimmy may appear at 35 mph which may mean that the idler arm is loose, which, in turn, beats up the worm and sector shaft. In 1958, the recirculating ball-type steering gear was fitted to overcome this problem. Cars with power steering did not have the problem, however.

Brake wheel cylinders may seize on a car that has been idle a long time. Check erratic braking. Many owners now use silicone brake fluid, which is not hydroscopic.

If the exhaust system is rusting, check carefully on the side of the heat riser where first damage usually occurs.

On 1955 to 1957 models, an obscure problem might occur in which the choke does not open properly. A tube on the inlet manifold might be burned through, which sucks exhaust into the automatic choke. The choke valve may then stick with carbon and dirt.

Some of the early 239 ci engines had camshaft problems and parts can be hard to find. Early engines have often been replaced by later blocks which, apart from numbers, are indistinguishable.

Also, check the front cross-member for rust, especially where the lower suspension arms attach.

Summary and prospects

The 1955 and 1956 Fords have been targeted by collectors, and prices have skyrocketed. The top of the market, as usual, is the Sunliner convertible, for which prices have long been five figures for fine examples. Prices for superb specimens may be as high as $40,000. But keep in mind that there are a lot of convertibles out there; production in 1955 was 49,966 units and in 1956, 58,147. Still, many are offered at modest prices that can give good service. It is the cost of restoration that brings those premium prices. The low-mileage, original, one-owner car is becoming harder to find and, even if not pristine, is regarded by some collectors as more desirable than the perfectly restored car.

The Country Sedan for 1955 was very popular and 106,284 units were sold. Prices are comparable to sedans with superb examples, approaching $5,000. Many good ones can still be bought for much lower prices, however.

Next in value is the Crown Victoria, with its distinctive center "roll bar." In 1955, 33,165 were built, but production fell dramatically in 1956 to 9,209. These 1956 models will be worth more. The plexiglass-top models will bring an even higher premium, since 1,999 were built in 1955 and only 603 in 1956. Owners of these cars have formed a special fraternity. The true pillarless Victoria is also very popular.

Prices are much lower for the closed cars, and good examples can be found in the $3,000 range. The ranch wagons, Country Sedans and Country Squires bring a slightly higher premium than the closed sedans, but not nearly as high as the earlier all-wood station wagons of 1946 to 1948. Wagons had become commonplace and were replacing the sedan for family use.

The enthusiasm for the 1955 and 1956 cars among collectors is well-placed, for these cars are easy to live with and maintain and have fine performance. Ford paid much attention to style and trim, and the cars' luxurious feeling was evident. Appreciation has been steady, and the future prospects for this series are excellent.

Production:

1955 1,451,157
1956 1,408,478

Auction prices

1955 Crown Victoria (1)	$12,250
1955 Sunliner (1)	$18,500
1955 Fairlane Crown Victoria (2)	$8,500
1955 Fordor (2)	$4,700
1956 Fairlane convertible (2)	$14,500

This 1956 Customline Victoria is the top value car below the Fairlane series and could bring $7,000 or more. Sales reached 33,130 which makes this model relatively rare. Upscale buyers preferred the Fairlane series as do collectors today. The V-8 emblem on the front fender indicates a 272 engine.

This 1956 Customline ranch wagon was one of seven wagons and is one step up from the basic Mainline version. A decent example would bring $4,000 to $5,000 and is a practical collectible. The top of the wagon market is the Parklane series with upgraded trim and carpets which can bring a 50 percent premium. The Country Squires with the wooden appliques will fall in between.

The 1956 Fairlane Victoria was immensely popular and 177,735 were sold. This is a preproduction model because the V-8 emblem on the front fender was used only on the Mainline and Customline series to identify the 272 engine, not available in the Fairlane which used the 292 or 312 engine and had the T-Bird emblem. Top prices for this model are now over $10,000. However, the Crown version with the strong central pillar is the target Victoria for collectors, perhaps because only 9,209 were sold. At the pinnacle of this Victoria market are the Crown models with the glass top, where prices have now passed $20,000. Rarity is surely a factor here—only 603 were built.

Chapter 5

Thunderbird 1955-1957

History

Ford's greatest product of the post-1945 collectibles was the Thunderbird, which profoundly influenced succeeding car design. It captured the attention of product developers and produced various spin-offs. Engine development was also spurred by the Thunderbird. Even the unit design of the 1958 Lincoln was made somewhat compatible with the 1958 Thunderbird, and both were built at the same plant.

The T-Bird's styling influence was im-

Here is a prototype 1955 T-Bird, photographed in the summer of 1954. The "eyebrows" over the headlights were modified for production. It is easy to see why this car was an instantly smashing success. A car in this condition today would bring as much as $30,000, a tenfold increase over the original price. Even with inflation, the Thunderbird has proven to be a great investment.

mense. The attraction of this new car was immediate and extraordinary, and has never waned. Used-car values of the early sixties show the Thunderbird retaining value beyond all other cars. For example, in 1962 the five-year-old 1957 Thunderbird was selling for sixty-one percent of its new price. The Corvette was valued at only forty-five percent of its new price. Even the mighty 1957 Mercedes 300SL was pulling only fifty-four percent of its new price in 1962.

Production of the Thunderbird began in September 1954. It had been shown on February 20, 1954, at the Detroit Auto Show, and from the response it was clear that history was in the making. Production started slowly and 1955 specifications followed the standard Ford line. However, a larger 292 ci 193 bhp engine was fitted, accelerating the horsepower race and setting the tone for future power leadership within Ford models.

Twelve-volt electrics were standard in 1956 and were a great improvement. In late 1956, the automatic transmission was water-cooled.

Engine options increased dramatically in 1957 with high-performance, racing and supercharger options. Improvements for 1957 included a twenty-gallon gasoline tank (up from fifteen gallons) with a side filler so that it was no longer necessary to tilt the Continental kit to fill the tank. The radio was partially transistorized. The instrument panel was redesigned with circular gauges, which in turn were given steady needle indicators. The dash was fully padded.

By 1957, about ninety percent were produced with automatic transmission, six percent with three-speed and four percent with three-speed with overdrive.

Production ended on December 13, 1957. Late 1957s were offered in 1958 colors.

Identification

1955: The model had the spare tire mounted horizontally in the trunk. Continental kits may have been added by owners after sale but are not common. There was no porthole in the hardtop. In 1955, a crossed flag and a Ford medallion were used front and rear; in 1956 and 1957 a Thunderbird medallion was fitted on the front.

1956: This had a Continental kit as standard, which had to be tilted to reach the fuel

When one opens the hood of a Thunderbird, it is nice to find this dress-up kit—accessory brightwork which adds to the appearance of the engine compartment. The 6-volt battery is big but still marginal for easy starting. The 12-volt system introduced in 1956 is much superior.

The regular gas pump appears to be mounted on grass in this pastoral setting. The smiling attendant seems to be reassuring the driver that no oil is needed, which, in combination with the regular gas pump, is suggesting economical motoring. The engine is in standard form without the dress-up kit.

filler. A rectangular outside air vent was mounted on the kickpanel just ahead of the door. The porthole appeared in the 1956 hardtop as a no-cost option which continued into 1957. The steering wheel had a recessed center and the hood medallion had wings.

1957: It had a vertical-mounted spare in the trunk, rear fender blades which extended forward over the door handles and a new bumper design without the two bullet-type guards of 1955-56. The instrument panel in 1957 contained individual gauges set in round bezels, like the 1956 passenger car.

There were seven engine series used in the 1955-57 Thunderbird. The code letter of each engine type leads off the serial number.

1955: P, 292 ci V-8 with the four-barrel carburetor used on all production.

1956: M, 292 ci V-8 with four-barrel carburetor used on standard transmission—the basic specification.

P, 312 ci V-8 with four-barrel carburetor used on automatic, standard and standard overdrive transmissions.

1957: C, 292 ci V-8 with two-barrel carburetor used on standard transmission—the basic specification.

D, 312 ci V-8 with four-barrel carburetor used on automatic and overdrive transmissions. (Ninety percent were automatics.) On January 23, 1957, fifteen D-types were fitted with McCulloch blowers and are popularly referred to as "DFs." The serial numbers will be near 30000.

E, 312 ci V-8 with two four-barrel carburetors for all transmissions. There were approximately 2,100 of these high-performance engines produced.

F, 312 ci V-8 with four-barrel carburetor and McCulloch VR57 supercharger. A special head reduced compression to 8.5:1. Production of the 196 F engines began in the spring. They were available at a factory invoice of $340. There were three grooves on the crank pulley and the manual transmission cars used two belts for the supercharger. With an automatic, the front groove was larger and drove the supercharger with a

It is unusual to see a Thunderbird without rear fender skirts. This 1955 model has the regular hardtop without portholes.

single belt. Power steering was only available on the automatic.

Caution: Some T-Birds with an F letter beginning the serial number do not have the blower, special heads or manifolds. Quite a few of the original buyers removed the blowers because they were noisy and not oil-tight. Today, the F-type blower and setup can be bought for about $5,000, and some T-Birds have been upgraded or re-equipped. When shopping for a blown T-Bird, carefully check the serial number and equipment to ensure originality.

Also, remember that a Ford dealer in 1957 would usually have been willing to add a supercharger to a D or E 312 ci engine, and similarly would have removed one from an F-series if the customer demanded it. Thus the formal total of 211 superchargers in the D and F series is an approximation.

The American Road T-Bird Club (Box 424, Dearborn, Michigan 48121) will supply a copy of the original invoice for most 1955s and all 1956s and 1957s for a fee, a useful service for checking authenticity. This service is available only to members of the Classic Thunderbird Club International.

Utility and performance

The T-Bird remains a joy to drive. The seating is a bit flat and legroom is limited, but owners rarely complain. The T-Bird remains a practical personal car, reliable and with sparkling performance. Many are still in daily service and, with the abundance of parts available, would appear to have an unlimited future.

The 1955 models had a somewhat harsher ride, however, because of stiffer springs.

Problem areas

As with new models, the 1955 T-Bird presented the most problems of the series. The 6-volt electrical system of the 1955 model occasionally produces hard starting. The early Holley carburetor tended to flood and was soon redesigned into a more compact unit. The door latches have caused problems, and replacements cost about $200.

The 1956 Thunderbird had a new hood medallion, side vents, portholes in the hardtop and the Continental kit, just visible in this picture. Prices will be higher for this series than for the 1955s. Twelve-volt electrics help. Some buyers like the Continental kit, which frees up trunk space.

The mufflers were mounted close to the floor, which can cause cabin heating. The vent doors in the 1956 helped cool the interior. The early push-button radio was inferior to the Town and Country models which appeared in 1956.

The add-on Continental kits of 1955 and the 1956 standard kit are awkward to use and reduce trunk access. It is almost impossible to change a tire without marking the sheet-metal tire cover. Fuel-filling requires the folding back of the kit—a nuisance. The Continental kit, especially the accessory add-on units, extended a substantial weight at the rear causing oversteer and fishtailing.

The frame was strengthened in 1956 to combat flexing. Check door fit on early models for chafing and evidence of frame distortion.

Oil consumption and smoky exhaust may be caused by blocked drain holes in the rocker-arm chambers—an easy fix. This problem may show as a rocker-cover gasket leak at the rear of the engine.

T-Birds also tend to overheat, caused by a combination of high power, small radiator and small water pump. Owners often fit thicker radiator cores.

In shopping for a T-Bird, it is crucial to check for missing parts which are becoming quite expensive. A jack or an air cleaner will cost upward of $200. A radio will run from $250 to $400.

Accessory items in the original specification, usually necessary for top prices, have often been fitted by restorers, but these items are becoming hard to find. This is especially true for power accessories. Power steering will cost about $1,500 or more. Power windows have run about $1,000 but are very hard to find, as are power seats which range from $500 to $600. Thus, the desirability of finding a car fully equipped is obvious.

The 1957 Thunderbird was restyled and the cleanliness of the new grille and bumper arrangement is evident. The rear fender blades were also a nice touch. The 1957s bring top money among the two-seater T-Birds and may be the highest priced of all post-1945 Fords.

Summary and prospects

The T-Bird market has shown a very substantial price increase in the last ten years, as the cars have moved into top collectibility status. There seems to be little doubt that steady appreciation will continue. The top prices for *any* year will normally require the full complement of accessories available at the time, such as the engine dress-up kit, both tops, fender shields, power steering, power windows, power brakes, back-up lights and tinted glass. There seems to be no discernible difference in price between automatic and stick shifts.

Prices for 1955 Thunderbirds will start as low as $6,000 for poor-running examples and range upward to $25,000 or $30,000. Top prices today may exceed $35,000.

The 1956 models will start at perhaps $8,000. The average market for fine examples is in the $27,000 to $33,000 range, with a few rare sales even above $40,000. (Highest prices usually include the 312 ci engine.) An exceptional sale at $75,000 occurred recently.

The 1957 models command top prices, beginning at about $10,000 for unrestored running cars to over $40,000 for perfect and authentic examples. The very rare supercharged F-type T-Bird will bring extraordinary prices, up to $60,000, and even good unrestored examples sell in the $30,000 range. Collectors have appreciated the 1957 instrument panel which was superior to the earlier models.

Occasionally, investors, indeed fanatics, will go *all out* in restoring a T-Bird. The availability of body and trim parts and almost all mechanical parts makes such a restoration attractive. There are few cars on the market today that have such high values and such an abundance of spares. The upward movement of the market is all the more remarkable because very few Thunderbirds have been voluntarily junked. The car was recognized as a collectible virtually as soon as production ceased in 1957, even though some dealers still had new 1957 Birds for sale in the spring of 1958.

There are a lot of Thunderbirds, which leads one to believe a car may be bought cheaply. But as time passes, the value of this outstanding collectible is more apparent, and longtime owners may have inflated opinions of their cars.

The pleasure of ownership is great, and the specialty clubs make for fun and tremendous availability of information. Few cars offer such handsome returns along with total reliability and pride of ownership.

Production:

1955 16,155
1956 15,631
1957 21,380

Auction prices

1955 T-Bird (1)	$31,000
1955 T-Bird (1)	$16,250 L
1955 T-Bird (2)	$20,000
1956 T-Bird (1)	$32,400
1956 T-Bird (1)	$17,000 L
1956 T-Bird (2)	$25,000
1956 T-Bird (2)	$13,100 L
1957 T-Bird (1)	$34,500
1957 T-Bird (1)	$10,000 L
1957 T-Bird (2)	$27,000
1957 T-Bird (2)	$12,200 L

The instrument panel of the 1957 Thunderbird is regarded as the best of the early series. Though designed in modified form for the 1955 Thunderbird, it was first used in the 1956 standard production.

Chapter 6

1957-1959

History

The 1957 was an all-new car, longer, lower and much bigger. There were two basic series: First, the Custom and Custom 300, which were built on the 116 inch short wheelbase. Second, the Fairlane and Fairlane 500, which were built on the 118 inch long wheelbase. The various station wagons and the Ranchero used the 116 inch wheelbase.

The Galaxie was new as a top-of-the-line series introduced in mid-1959. The two convertibles were listed there exclusively. The Custom was soon dropped, and the following year the Custom 300 was also dropped as the Fairlane descended to the bottom of the lineup.

An exceptional novelty for the three-year series was the hardtop retractable convertible, called the Skyliner, a name borrowed from the plexiglass-top Victoria of 1954. (The 1955 and 1956 Crown Victorias with transparent tops are sometimes incorrectly

The Fairlane 500 Victoria Club had the high rear chrome fin and sports turbine wheel covers as used on the Thunderbird. The long 122 inch wheelbase carried the new bulk with grace. This very popular car found 183,202 buyers in 1957 and it remains a fine collectible. Prices can reach as high as $7,500 for outstanding examples.

referred to as Skyliners.)

There was an expansion of color in 1957 with seventeen hues, a cutback to twelve in 1958, and then no less than twenty-four colors in 1959.

Identification

1957: Fourteen-inch wheels began. Front A-pillar sloped downward to the rear. Radiator opening covered by a grille with long rectangular spaces delineated with narrow chrome bars.

1958: "Mouth" of the grille extended well forward, with hexagonal openings. The effect was heavy and is considered the least attractive of the three-year production period.

The new big-block FE engine was introduced. The 332 ci version was offered in the Ford Fairlane 500, with the 352 ci Interceptor as an option. Since engine size and power affect value in the sixties cars, buyers need to confirm what is being offered, especially since casual exterior identification will not help, particularly with the big-block engines. (See the Appendix for more engine specifications.)

Buyers usually familiarize themselves with

This 1957 Custom 300 Fordor on the short 116 inch wheelbase was a good-looking family sedan. A whopping 194,877 were sold, the largest of any body style. The full-length chrome trim with gold anodized center provided flash. Nice examples of this car sell for around $3,500.

the engine codes on the data or patent plate found on the left-front door pillar or at the base of the windshield. In addition, when exceptional claims are made by the seller, a check on the engine's casting numbers is useful. Even then, parts can be swapped, from the obvious valve cover and manifolds to more subtle components such as heads. A 352 engine can readily masquerade as a more desirable 427 engine.

In a restoration, engines are often the least expensive part of the job. The heavy expenditures occur in paint and trim. Hence, in appraising a car do not be unduly swayed by engine claims, especially since high-performance trim kits can be added to an engine at a low cost by unscrupulous sellers.

1959: Galaxie series had little stars set in the radiator opening. A profusion of slash stripes and trim decorated the sides of the cars. As a general rule, the absence of script plates or model identification means that the car is the lowest-priced custom series.

Utility and performance

Even with the smaller Y-block, the Fairlanes were fast. A long-distance record of 108 mph for 50,000 miles was established at Bonneville beginning September 9, 1956, and ending September 28. This record run used a 312 ci engine rated at 270 bhp, the most powerful unsupercharged rating in standard tune.

By comparison, the big-block 352 ci engine with mechanical valve lifters rated 300 bhp (but was actually lower). Hydraulic lifters were fitted after a couple of months of production. The 390 ci engine, so widely fitted in the sixties, was ready but not used because of Ford's agreement with the American Manufacturers Association not to race.

Problem areas

These cars were tough and long-lasting. In the Cruise-O-Matic transmission from 1958 to 1966, chatter in reverse gear may indicate a broken case. The center support

The fabulous Skyliner retractable hardtop has an enthusiastic following and prices can reach $20,000. However, good examples may be found in the $12,000 to $15,000 range. This particular 1957 prototype had reversed two-tone colors, the more typical specification being the light color on top.

could crack under heavy use.

The fresh-air inlet at the base of the windshield drains to beneath the car through a rubber tube. If the tube fails, water drains to the interior floor. Moisture will be held under the carpets or especially under rubber mats, which in either case causes rust.

Additional problems for cars of this period may be found in the preceding chapter.

Summary and prospects

There are many collectors who find cars among this series the greatest collectible Fords of them all. Members of the Fabulous Fifties Ford Club of America often mark the 1957 the central target car of the fifties. One of the reasons may be that there were so many sold in that banner year; Ford beat Chevrolet by some 165,000 units. The 1959 is a better car mechanically, and other collectors find it exceptionally beautiful. In any event, prices for these cars have been strong.

However, few collectors are restoring closed cars of this period, perhaps because many have survived and some may still be found with relatively low mileage. Such cars have made splendid parts sources for restoration of the more exotic models.

Prices can still be low for sedans, in the $1,000 to $2,000 range. Runners can sometimes be bought for three figures. But the minute a very clean low-mileage car appears, the collectors gather and prices will rise as high as the $4,000 level. The Victoria pillar-

The 1957 Country Sedan used the Custom 300 side trim. It is a very useful car, but values are no higher than a sedan. Nice average examples can still be found in the $2,500 range.

less models of any series will bring a premium.

Collector interest centers on the two open models. The Sunliner convertible (four stars) is exceptionally pretty and is much sought after. Excellent examples are selling in the $15,000 range, with occasional sales at even higher prices. Good serviceable runners in decent shape may be found for around $10,000, with the occasional bargain at lower figures.

A very specialized market applies to the Skyliner retractable hardtop model, which should be rated five stars. This car has a special club and a devoted following. Prices have been very strong, generally above the Sunliner, with superb show examples in the $20,000 range. But many can be bought for less that are in very nice shape. Buyers need to be careful that the top mechanism is functioning properly.

Membership in the Skyliner Retractable Club is recommended in order to become thoroughly acquainted with this unusual car. Serious buyers will then quickly find trustworthy sellers and fair prices.

The 1958 cars are generally regarded with less favor by collectors because of their rather awkward bulbous grille. Opinion is about equally divided on the relative merits of the 1957 and 1959 models.

Any open car in this three-year period will be a fine bet for long-term appreciation and will give immense satisfaction and pride of ownership.

Production:

1957 1,655,068
1958 950,053
1959 1,394,684

Auction prices

1957 Skyliner retractable (1)	$18,600
1957 Skyliner retractable (2)	$8,500 L
1957 Fairlane 500 convertible (2) ...	$11,500
1958 Skyliner retractable (1)	$10,500
1959 Skyliner retractable (1)	$24,250

The 1957 Country Squire has collectible value but buyers are not easy to find. A perfect specimen might reach $6,000; good examples are available at much less.

The 1957-59 Ford Ranchero is a very strong collectible because *only* for these three years was the full-size Ford chassis used. In 1960 the Ranchero series was moved to the Falcon line. This 1957 model was the bottom of the line but sported a grille guard. Even so, an average example is an easy $2,500. Superb Rancheros are not easy to find because so many did hard work, but if a splendid example comes along it could earn $6,000 to $7,000.

The standard Fairlane on the long wheelbase carried this side trim, generally not as desirable as the 500 series. Decent sedans like this can be readily found under $2,000.

This 1958 Sunliner is a beauty and is shown with the dark color on top, unusual for 1958. These cars will sell at prices slightly below the 1957s and 1959s. Good usable examples can still be found for around $10,000.

A 1958 Fairlane Fordor had side trim something like the Corvette. Cars like this do not rate high in collectibility and may be found for around $1,500 for good-running clean examples.

A really superb 1957 Fairlane 500 Sunliner convertible is approaching $20,000 in value. This example had the standard wheel covers and the usual two-tone paint arrangement. Sunliners in good condition can still be found in the $12,000 to $14,000 range, and their future seems bright.

The first Galaxie, built in 1959, had the Thunderbird-style roof. The name "Fairlane" still appeared on the trunk. The Club Victoria is very collectible and prices are the highest of all the closed cars, upwards of $7,000 and beyond.

This 1959 Fairlane 500 had the Galaxie Thunderbird roofline but should not be confused with a Galaxie. It is still a popular collectible, with prices right below the Galaxie.

Chapter 7

Thunderbird 1958-1960

★★★★

History

The decision for the four-seater Thunderbird was made in early 1956. The unit construction was more suited to the new 113 inch wheelbase of the Thunderbird than that of the bigger Lincoln, both of which would share production facilities at the new Wixom plant. Production of the coupe began January 13, 1958, and the convertible on April 15. Deliveries did not begin until June.

Sales were very heavy, especially in light of the generally poor record for the industry in 1958. *Motor Trend* awarded the title "Car of the Year" to the new four-passenger Thunderbird.

The new big-block 352 ci engine was standard in the Thunderbird. The 430 ci engine used in the Lincoln became available

The 1958 four-passenger Thunderbird was a great success and it turned out to be a tough runner. The welded body made it ideal for demolition derbies and many were lost. Recently, prices have risen rapidly. Excellent coupes are breaking $10,000, and outstanding convertibles are exceeding $20,000. Poor examples will sell for much less, though, because restoration costs are high.

in 1959. Also in 1959, leaf springs replaced the rear coils which had originally been designed to accommodate an air suspension.

The sunroof hardtop was offered *only* in 1960.

Identification

1958: "Chicken wire" grille both front and rear with five bars on the rear bulge plus two taillights on each side.

1959: Rear bars and a spear on the side and two taillights on each side. The grille has horizontal bars.

1960: Three hash marks on the rear fender and three taillights on each side.

Utility and performance

The 1958-60 four-seaters had more of a sporting feeling than the later models, even though the seats were upright and had little lateral support. Development of the Thunderbird usually moved toward a softened ride. Performance of an early prototype tested by *Motor Trend* was 0-60 mph in 13.5 seconds, though Tom McCahill reported 0-60 mph in 9.9 seconds.

The big 430 ci engine offered in 1959 and 1960 gave impressive performance but added a little weight up front and further degraded

Ford advertising described the 1958 Thunderbird instrument panel as having an "unmistakable sports car personality" though no tachometer is in sight. The glovebox door is shown open because it was "ingeniously designed to serve as a convenient service tray."

There was little outward change in the 1959 model, though the new grille motif was especially neat. There were many other refinements, however, and collectors have tended to favor that year. Prices will be strong and rising. A record $30,000 was paid for an exceptional 1959 convertible in a recent auction, but there are ordinary examples at half the price.

handling. Braking power was weak with only 175 inches of lining, twelve square inches greater than that of Ford's first hydraulics in 1939. The Thunderbird had added a thousand pounds and was much faster than that nimble 1939 pony car.

Though gasoline mileage will be modest, the 1958-60 Thunderbirds are splendid drivers and give much pleasure.

Problem areas

As with new models, the 1958s have more problems than later cars. The rear coil springs of the 1958 have weakened over the years and replacement is increasingly difficult. The leaf spring models in 1959 and 1960 are much better.

The radio speaker faced upward in the console in 1958 through 1960. Heat and light take their toll on the speaker cones. This is true of Ford models in general during the fifties.

Electrical troubles may appear because circuitry was growing ever more complex and, with time, decay is inevitable. For example, in 1958 and 1959 the convertible rear deck was unlocked electrically and then opened by hand so that the top could be raised. Little trouble is experienced in these systems. In 1960, however, the convertible top mechanism was fully automatic and has had more breakdowns.

Summary and prospects

The survival of these first-series square four-seater T-Birds has been only fair. The

There was no mistaking the Thunderbird profile. Buyers flocked to this distinctive car, and 57,195 copies of this hardtop were sold in 1959.

Production of all four-seater T-Birds vastly outnumbered the earlier two seater.

sheet metal was welded between 1958 and 1960, which made the bodies extra strong and thus very desirable for use in demolition derbies; a great many T-Birds perished in such competition. There was no leather in 1958 and air-conditioning was uncommon, especially in the convertibles. The style of the 1958 grille is not as highly regarded by most collectors as the 1959. For a long time these early cars were not sought after.

The 1958s, 1959s and 1960s were low priced until about 1984, when substantial appreciation began. Restored coupes now bring $8,000 to $10,000, while excellent convertibles range from $15,000 to $25,000.

The 1959 model has found great favor among collectors and leads the market in the early square T-Bird group. The many running changes improved this car greatly. Leather was available. The top was semi-automatic, though the rear deck needed to be opened by hand. The record price for a 1959 convertible has reached $30,000, with prices for fine examples around $20,000.

Trim changes for 1960 made this model even gaudier. The top was fully automatic. A sunroof was available in 1960, which raises value as does the big 430 ci engine. (There were only 377 coupes with both options.)

Enthusiastic club support makes these early square four-passenger Thunderbirds a desirable collectible. Steady appreciation may be expected in the near future. Ownership can give both pride and utility.

Production:	*hardtop*	*convertible*
1958	35,758	2,134
1959	57,195	10,261
1960	78,447	11,860*

**2,536 with sunroof*

Auction prices

1958 T-Bird (2)	$6,800
1959 T-Bird (1)	$21,000
1959 T-Bird (1)	$8,000 L
1959 T-Bird (2)	$19,250
1960 T-Bird (1)	$11,500
1960 T-Bird (2)	$10,000

The 1960 Thunderbird had a fussy grille, some egregious trim and a nice optional sunroof. Prices are going up on this fine collectible, with excellent hardtops in the $10,000 range and convertibles around $20,000.

1960

Chapter 8

Galaxie 1960-1972

★

History

The Galaxie name was introduced in 1959 for the top of the line, replacing the Fairlane 500 which, in turn, had replaced the Crestline in 1955. This completely new body style of 1960 commonly begins the decade of the Galaxie.

The rounded style of 1960 was a break from the square motifs of 1959. The very sharp horizontal fins were typical of the bizarre styling of the industry during this period, but were quickly muted the following year and had disappeared by 1962. The perimeter-type frame was new and gave solid support to much bigger bodies.

The restyling for 1961 was extensive and brought a General Motors look to the Ford grille, in which the 1958-59 Buick pattern was followed. In 1962, the 500 XL model was introduced, XL standing for "extra lively," in

An early factory picture of the 1960 Fairlane 500. The 1959 "Fairlane" script was still on the rear fender but was moved to the front for production. Gunsights were added to the crown of the front fender. This new style featured the sharp horizontal rear fins. Sedans such as this have modest collecting value and poor examples are still being used as parts cars.

part because the 406 ci 4V and 6V engines replaced the 390 in this series. The XL line was offered in the two-door hardtop and convertible body styles. In 1963, the fastback style appeared and was instantly popular. The 427 engine was available in that year also.

The convertible history in this period had changes. Convertibles in the Fairlane 500 and 500 XL appeared in 1966, paralleled by the upscaled Galaxie 500 and XL. The Fairlane 500 convertible continued through 1969. The 500 XL became the Torino GT in 1968. The Galaxie XL became the Ford XL in 1968, which continued through 1970. The LTD then replaced it in 1971.

When buying big Ford convertibles of this period, it is always good to find the top-of-the-line car for any given year. But condition will override all other factors.

Identification

For the sixties, an easy check on year is the first digit on the VIN, or Vehicle Identification Number. (0=1960, 1=1961 and so on.)

Galaxies have certain sheet-metal characteristics that may help to identify quickly. Check photographs. Look for "Galaxie" nameplate.

1960: A very sharp horizontal rear fender blade, half-circular taillight reflected by bumper cutout.

1961: Round taillights and small fins.

1962: Fins are gone, broad single molding stripe, bumper cutout for taillights.

1963: Two molding stripes, vertical bars on rear fender by taillight.

1964: Power-tapered body lines, single spear beginning at front headlamps tapering into molding stripe in middle of front door.

1965: Dual headlamps mounted vertically—no slash stripe, unified single motif bars in grille.

1966: Grille divided into two sections.

1967: Rear fender line has hump.

1968: Grille divided in middle—dual headlamps horizontal.

1969: Strong lower belt molding with brightwork beneath (at hubcap level).

1970: Center bar in grille divided into two fine bars.

1971: Grille grid massed in center.

The Galaxie was fitted with numerous engines, which can affect value. Before buying, review the Appendix on engines for some familiarity with the options.

This 1961 Galaxie four-door Victoria was a handsome car and prices today for excellent copies are climbing. Good examples are in the $2,500 to $4,000 range. Ford used the term Town for four-door hardtops and Club for two-door hardtops.

Performance and utility

Armed with the colossal big-block engines, Ford became a major competitor in track events. In 1962, Ford won ten out of twenty-two United States Auto Club (USAC) races.

In quarter-mile drag racing, Ford's best times broke under twelve seconds and exceeded 120 mph. In October 1962, a supertuned Galaxie did 500 miles at 163.86 mph and had best top speed of 176.978 mph.

These extraordinary performances were possible because Ford offered a large number of speed and handling options, including nine different rear-end ratios, suspension stiffeners, heavy-duty driveline parts and so on.

The emphasis on speed in the Galaxie series ended in 1967 when it was realized that the smaller cars, particularly the Mustang, were better suited to high performance. The big Fords moved toward a luxury image with the LTD series, introduced in 1965.

In 1966 the 428 ci engine appeared as the 7-Liter model (actually 6.980 liters) with 345 bhp. The stroke was longer (3.98 in.) than

The 1961 Galaxie Starliner had a rakish rear quarter and is the most valuable of the closed cars for this year. A good example will bring about $3,500, while superb specimens will cost around $5,000.

The 1962 Galaxie Sunliner was a handsome car. This example sports the 390 ci engine. Big-engine convertibles will always be at the top level of collectibles, and prices for such a car in good shape begin around $5,000 and up.

the 427 (3.78 in.). Both engines were available through 1967. The 428 was available in 1968 and then was replaced by the 429 in 1969 which, by 1970, was rated at 360 bhp in maximum tune. The standard engine for the Galaxie at the end of the sixties was the 302, with an advertised 220 bhp.

Keep in mind that a big Galaxie, especially around 1964, may not be much of a handler in the sense of bright and crisp cornering and control. This will be especially true when shocks wear and front-end suspension becomes sloppy.

Problem areas

The Galaxie was a big tough car which had 100,000 mile reliability. It is uncommon for failures to occur in any major components. These cars seem to have the capacity to run forever with virtually no maintenance.

However, check out the lower struts on the front suspension—especially where they bolt up to the frame. In severe climates the bolting holes can rust and allow A-arm movement. Similar rust problems may appear at the frame above and behind the rear axle. Water and spray traps around wheel arches, deck lids and quarter panels should be examined. There are many good Galaxies still available from dry-climate areas and buyers will pay a little more for solid cars.

Summary and prospects

The Galaxie was not seen as a collectible car until recently, but enthusiasts are finding growing support. A Galaxie Club has focused attention and helped to improve its marketability.

The convertibles, as usual, have the highest value. Beginning in 1960, top specimens will bring as much as $12,000. With each succeeding year, convertible value drops and by the 1970 model is around $5,000. Always be on the lookout for XL versions after 1962, though, which will bring a premium. Appreciation for these cars has been around twenty percent in the past five years, in part because values were low around 1980. Future appreciation should be good.

The XL hardtop is another collectible body style, although prices are only seventy percent to eighty percent of what the convertibles will bring. Superb examples from the early sixties may bring as much as $7,000.

Here is a fiberglass Starlift roof fitted to a 1962 Galaxie 500 Sunliner, an item which was never factory produced. The wheel covers were from a 1962 Thunderbird.

Four-door hardtops have lesser value—except for the 1963 and 1964 XLs.

So far, closed bodies for the sixties have limited collectibility. Running cars in poor condition can still be bought for $1,000 or less. Clean low-mileage examples might well be "put away," though appreciation for closed cars will be modest. Some are still being junked.

This analysis also applies to standard production models. If a Galaxie shows up with a big engine and numerous competition options, the prices climb—even on closed cars. Interest in the muscle cars has increased dramatically in the eighties, and Ford's great 427 engine remains a target collectible. Buyers are cautioned to verify all engine and equipment claims beginning with a careful examination of the patent plate.

At the very top of the Galaxie market would be a *perfect* XL convertible with luxury equipment and the 390 engine, which together could produce a $20,000 collectible. An attractive alternate would be the 427 engine, but keep in mind that this engine was not mated with power equipment and luxury items.

Production of convertibles:

Year	Production	Year	Production
1960	44,762	*1967*	24,229
1961	44,614	*1968*	17,898
1962	55,829	*1969*	13,312
1963	55,427	*1970*	6,348
1964	52,480	*1971*	5,750
1965	41,779	*1972*	4,234
1966	33,824		

Auction prices

1962 Galaxie 500, 390 ci (2)	$1,800
1963 Galaxie 2-door hardtop (2)	$2,100
1964 Galaxie hardtop (1)	$5,500
1964 Galaxie hardtop (2)	$5,700
1964 Galaxie 500 XL convertible (2)	$4,400
1965 Galaxie 500 (2)	$1,150
1966 Galaxie 500 XL coupe (2)	$3,550

The garden-variety 1962 Galaxie two-door club sedan. This car can still be bought below $1,000, and some remain in daily use. They were tough cars.

The 1962 Galaxie 500 XL hardtop with desirable bucket seats. There were 28,412 of these built in 1962. The market begins at around $2,000, with prices much higher for fine examples.

A 1963 Galaxie 500 Club Victoria with the 390 ci engine. These Victorias always bring more money than pillared sedans but less than the XL edition. Prices will vary widely depending on condition, from $1,000 up to about $3,500.

This 1963 four-door hardtop 500 XL had either a 352 or 289 engine because there are no flag medallions on the car. A flag carried the designation 390, or 406 or 427 engine. This was the first year for the amber turn signals. A good example of this car might bring around $2,000.

This fine 1964 Galaxie 500 XL convertible had the 390 ci engine and is the target car of this year for collectors. It was the last year for the strong X frame. Fine examples bring around $6,000 or more.

The Los Angeles-issued license plate suggests a southern California beach site for this shot of a 1964 Galaxie 500 XL convertible. It had the 390 ci engine. This was the last year for the strong X frame. Fine examples bring around $6,000 or more.

The 1965 Galaxie 500 XL hardtop, with a Michigan ZZ plate, was posed in front of a pretty suburban home. The two headlamps were mounted in a vertical plane and continued through 1967. Prices for this series may be slightly lower than for the earlier cars, but good convertibles with the 390 ci engine will bring strong prices.

The 1965 Galaxie 500 XL with the 390 ci engine was a bigger car than in 1964. The sculptured sides of the 1964 car gave way to smoother surface development. Prices for this car in average shape start at around $4,000 and climb with condition to around $6,000. This could be the bargain big convertible of the decade.

This 1966 Galaxie 500 XL convertible had the diecast grille, as did the LTD and the 428 ci engine 7-Liter. This car had the 390 ci engine. The changes were few from 1965 and values are about the same.

The 1966 four-door Custom 500 had a stamped aluminum grille. There were 109,449 units of this one body style and model produced. The value for this car is low, perhaps not more than $1,000. Collectors prefer hardtops and convertibles.

The 1967 Galaxie 500 XL convertible had another diecast steel grille. The big visual difference was the hump in the rear fender. This car had the 428 engine, according to the insignia on the front fender. Big engines usually mean bigger prices.

The four-door 1968 Galaxie was a tough solid car and many are still in service. They have little collectible value and many have been used for parts in restoring more exotic body styles. A 1968 sedan can be bought for under $1,000.

This 1968 Galaxie 500 convertible had the 390 ci engine. This would be a good car for an entry-level long-range investment since prices in this year and for the 1969 models are about as low as any full-size convertible of the sixties. Running examples requiring renovation can start at $2,000 with prices topping around $5,000.

This 1969 Galaxie two-door hardtop had the big 429 ci engine, new for the year. It was a great and fast car, very near the end of the heavy muscle cars. They may well have future collectibility. Despite their performance, some of these closed cars are still being junked. However, on a sheer investment growth basis, this sort of car may offer great profit.

The 1970 Galaxie was hardly distinguishable from the 1969 and the same collecting strategy applies. The Ford XL convertible was available for the last time in 1970 and would be the more usual target car for collectors.

A cutaway show version of the 429 Boss engine with exhaust headers and special valve covers. This was the final big engine from Ford in the sixties and had full pressure to the lifters plus all journals. It was a clean-burning engine and was better able to cope with growing smog restraints. The crescent-shaped combustion chamber was similar to a hemi-head. This engine was available for NASCAR competition and then in street versions for the 1969 and 1970 Mustangs.

Chapter 9

LTD 1967-1972

★

History

The top of the line for the 500 Galaxie two- and four-door hardtops was first called the LTD in 1965. Luxury trim and vinyl tops almost always marked the LTD. In 1966, the 428 ci 345 bhp engine powered the new Galaxie 500 7-Liter series, in which the LTD was again at the top for hardtop-trim models.

The LTD was gradually breaking away from the Galaxie line, and was essentially a separate model by 1967 when a four-door sedan was added. There were few changes in 1968, but in 1969 the new short-stroke 429 engine was fitted in the LTD and continued in 1970.

The era of the big engines was passing. The mighty 427 was gone by the end of 1967. The 428s were through at the end of 1970. The 429 would linger on into the seventies, but power was deemphasized—not

This rare 1966 LTD limousine had the 390 ci engine. The hardtop configuration on a stretched body may have been unique and speaks well for the torsional rigidity of the chassis. There are so few survivors of this limousine that an estimation of value is difficult, but collectors will surely find something of interest here.

only by Ford's marketing designs but by emission controls. The withdrawal from performance directed the focus to luxury, and the LTD prospered.

Of particular interest to collectors is the listing of the convertible to the LTD series in 1971 and 1972, that last of the big Ford open cars. As shown by the production statistics, few were produced.

There is one other elusive rarity in the LTD line—namely the limousine built in 1966 and fitted with the 390 ci engine.

Identification

The big LTDs were on a 121 inch wheelbase. The LTD nameplate will be found in various places.

Performance and utility

The big-engine LTDs were well able to cope with the 4,000 pound weight, and performance was marvelous. Gasoline mileage was modest.

Problem areas

These big Fords have been subject to rust, especially in lower body areas as described in the Galaxie chapter. A check of *any* car is prudent. The big V-8 engines seem to have exceptionally long life; drivelines and transmissions are also strong. LTDs survive under great abuse.

Summary and prospects

The LTDs have not found heavy collector interest to date, apart from the convertibles. Many of the closed cars continue to be junked. Yet from time to time, an exceptional hardtop may bring several thousand dollars. Convertibles are still inexpensive, too, and poor specimens are offered more frequently than in any other Ford model. But again, a fine clean LTD convertible may bring $7,000 or more.

The very limited limousine production in the sixties makes appraisals of such cars difficult, but if one turns up, it surely should be collected.

There is an opportunity here for restorers. The long-term appreciation for LTDs should be gradual and steady, yet some can still be bought for near junk prices. Keep an eye out for the low-mileage, one-owner car, still quite possible in this series.

The LTD became a separate top-of-the-line model in 1967, and this four-door hardtop was the production leader with 51,978 sold. Though these cars are still being junked, good clean original examples may bring a couple of thousand dollars.

Production (convertible):
1971 5,750
1972 4,234

Auction prices	
1968 LTD 2-door (2)	$950
1969 LTD convertible (3)	$1,750
1970 LTD convertible, 429 ci (3)	$2,800

This 1967 LTD two-door hardtop had the big 428 ci engine and the short rear quarter window. Prices still do not justify full restoration costs and thus only fine original examples have value. Collectors of late sixties cars prefer the assured future of convertibles.

The 1968 LTD had hidden headlamps. The big 428 ci engine was still offered but soon gave way to the 429. Only a superb, clean example will have value.

The last "big" Ford convertibles in the collectible era were offered in the LTD series and in 1971 and 1972 looked like this. Because they were the "last," they have survived in large numbers though only 4,234 were built in 1972. Good ones will bring $5,000 and up.

This 1972 LTD two-door hardtop is a big handsome car which may still be bought cheaply. It may yet find a following though collectors usually concentrate on the convertible.

Chapter 10

Falcon 1960-1965

★

History

The new Falcon was introduced in October 1959 and was a smashing success. Ford's new small car weighed in at 2,289 pounds, well below the 3,585 pounds of the Fairlane six-cylinder. The Falcon engine displaced 144.3 ci and produced 90 bhp at 4200 rpm. It weighed only 345 pounds due to thin-wall casting and internal intake manifolding.

Sales success was instant, and development began. An optional engine giving 101 bhp was available in 1961, along with a Futura special two-door sedan. The Futura became a regular model in 1962, and in 1963 the then-new small-block V-8 became an option at 260 ci with 164 bhp.

This original Falcon of 1960 was the factory prototype; the front end was high, suggesting that an engine had not yet been installed. Such early Falcons have low collecting value. An original clean example could, however, be a good useable curiosity.

Important to collectors was the introduction of a convertible in 1963, available in three forms as the standard 76A, the Futura 76B and the 76B with Sprint trim. These convertibles were a stunning success. Production was 18,942 cars for the 76A, 12,250 for the 76B and 4,602 for the 76B Sprint.

An all-new body appeared in 1964. The convertible was offered in standard form with bench seats and sold 13,220 units, while 2,980 were sold with bucket seats. The Sprint with bucket seats sold 3,652 units while the rarest of the four types, the bench-seat Sprint, sold only 626 units. The last year for the Futura convertible was 1965; 6,191 were sold with bench seats and only 124 with bucket seats. The Mustang convertible was taking over.

In 1963 and 1964, the V-8 option specified the 260 engine with 164 bhp. In 1964 and 1965, the 289 engine was offered with as much as 271 bhp. A very few 289s were delivered in the 1964 model year. Weight was climbing and a loaded convertible exceeded 3,000 pounds. In 1964, fiberglass was used on all opening panels of the rally cars to bring down weight. A few 427 ci big-block engines were installed in racing and drag Falcons by specialist builders.

The Falcons for 1965 could be had with a 289 ci 200 hp engine. Thereafter, the performance emphasis would be on the Mus-

The 1961 Falcon had minor trim changes. It was a strong seller. These cars are still being junked and have not received much collector interest.

tang. For 1966, the Falcon was a shortened Fairlane and does not have as much collector interest.

An alternator was specified for 1965.

Identification

The simple Falcon styling of 1960 lasted three years with only minor grille and trim changes.

1963: Upper greenhouse restyled along with some sheet-metal changes.

1964: Car sides heavily restyled with a long wedge-shape motif, which continued through 1965.

1966: All-new body, sharing Fairlane styling and muting the original Falcon identity.

Utility and performance

Performance was modest until the introduction of the 260 ci V-8 engine in 1963,

This 1962 Falcon Futura had bucket seats and deluxe trim. It is beginning to have interest for collectors, and prices start at about $1,000, with excellent examples bringing perhaps twice as much.

with 164 bhp at 4400 rpm. This was followed by the 289 ci engine with a maximum 271 bhp in highest tune. With such low car weight, these big-engine Falcons were very fast and would point the way toward future high-performance development. By 1967, Ford was concentrating performance on small cars.

Problem areas

The 1960-61 Falcon front suspension requires adjustment from time to time—not a simple job because the upper control arms, on which the coil springs are mounted, are adjusted by shims. Ball joints can also wear.

The engine can sludge and screens can clog, in which case the valve gear may not get oil; the result is a noisy engine. Surviving Falcons usually have clean engines. In fact, any decent surviving Falcon has generally benefited from maintenance and care.

Summary and prospects

The early Falcon sedans have low collector value but continue to be good utility vehicles. However, the convertible models, and to a lesser extent the hardtops, have rapidly increasing value. The bigger 289 ci V-8 engine models and those with the Sprint options are at the top of the market. Look for the tachometer, bucket seats and center consoles, woodgrain steering wheel and chrome engine dress-up items.

Top condition big-engine Futura Sprint convertibles are approaching $10,000. Splendid Sprint hardtops may be as high as $8,000. More typical to this market, however, are very good condition convertibles at $4,000 to $5,000.

Good-running Falcon sedans can be bought for $1,000 or less, while top-condition Futura sedans could run as high as $2,500.

Apart from the Sprint Futura V-8s, appreciation of Falcons as a whole is uncertain.

Production:

1960 435,676 *1963* 328,339
1961 474,241 *1964* 300,770
1962 414,282 *1965* 213,601

Auction prices

1963 Falcon convertible (2)	$5,250
1964 Falcon convertible (2)	$4,500
1964 Falcon sprint 2-door hardtop (2)	$4,000
1965 Falcon sprint convertible (2)	$6,500

This 1963 Falcon Futura convertible had the six-cylinder engine but still rates as a solid collectible, with prices starting at around $3,000 on up to $6,000 or more. With the 260 ci V-8 engine, prices will be substantially higher.

In 1964, the sheet metal was changed and the Falcon had a more aggressive appearance. This Futura Sprint convertible had the 260 ci V-8 engine and was fitted with a tachometer under the windshield. This very desirable Falcon in top condition can bring as much as $8,000.

FALCONS

The 289 ci V-8 engine was offered in the Falcon in 1965 and was a strong performer. It was the last year of distinctive sheet metal for the Falcon, and the last year for the convertible. A Falcon Futura convertible with this big engine brings a strong price. After 1965, Falcons have less collector interest.

Chapter 11

Thunderbird 1961-1966

★★★

History

The Thunderbirds in this era are divided into two groups: the first, from 1961 to 1963, and the second, from 1964 to 1966. The convertible ended in 1966, a cutoff point for collectors. Also, the 1967 T-Bird had a smoothed roof quarter flowing gently into the rear deck, a radical change from all former T-Bird styles. The distinctive T-Bird look was fading.

The 1961 Thunderbird had the projectile look and picked up styling ideas from the 1960 Fairlane, especially in the front-fender profile. It was a handsome car and enjoyed strong sales. The price of these cars, historically lagging behind the 1958-60 T-Bird series, has recently shown sharp increases.

The first series, called by designer William Boyer the "projectile look," echoed themes from the 1960 Fairlane. In profile, there was a long, smooth crown line on the fender, rising neatly from a front midpoint and flowing backward to small rear blades. Great round taillamps were tucked beneath the rear blades.

The design had splendid unity. In 1962, a landau version was introduced with vinyl roof and landau bars on the rear quarter. Also new in 1962 was the roadster, with a fiberglass deck covering the back seating area, Kelsey-Hayes wire wheels, grab bar and distinctive emblems.

The second series Thunderbird returned to more angular shapes and again was a beautifully integrated design. It was a busier design than the first series because it combined themes of the square T-Bird of 1958 and the 1961 series. The flank of the car had a low molding. Two rectangular taillights were set beneath the two deck "pods," as designer Boyer called them.

In 1966, a Town Landau version was offered in which the rear quarter window was blanked and landau irons were applied to the blanked quarter. The heavy front bumpers on the 1964s gave way to a cleaner and lighter look in 1966.

The rectangular taillights were spread across the whole rear of the car. The rear fender skirts were optional, and in 1966 had stainless-steel trim on the lower edge of the skirt. Without skirts, stainless steel was used to trim the wheel arch.

Identification

A convenient way to identify the year quickly is by the side trim at the back of the rear fender.

1961: Four small horizontal bars center on the round taillight.

1962: Three thick bars mounted sequentially.

1963: Script "Thunderbird."

1964: No trim.

1965: Script "Thunderbird," long horizontal top to "T."

1966: Script "Thunderbird," bottom of "T" curled forward.

Upholstery style in mid-1962 was changed and continued through the 1963 models. The armrests became integral with the door panels.

Buyers looking for *genuine* roadster models should be very careful, as the parts necessary for a roadster conversion are readily available including the panels, headrests and passenger grab bar. Genuine roadsters begin with model numbers 76B instead of the usual 76A for convertibles.

The three bars on the rear fender identify this Thunderbird as a 1962 model. Beautiful coupes in the 1961-63 series can bring as much as $10,000.

It is possible that an authentic roadster may still contain the original factory order, a small piece of paper describing the car's makeup. It may be found tucked in the spring portion of the back seat, and will contain the phrase "tonneau job."

From September 1961 to February 1962 the serial number 2785Z is found on both convertibles and roadsters. After February 1962 the roadster serial number will be 2Y89Z.

Utility and performance

Handling for the 1961 was softer than the 1958-60 square Birds, and wallowing was reported. The problem was sufficiently serious so that in early 1962 twenty-five-pound weights were mounted on the four corners of the car to provide stability, a palliative that was quickly abandoned. Early models did not have the Swing-Away or "fat man's" steering wheel which became standard in 1962.

The first FM transistor radio appeared in 1963.

Zero to 60 mph time of 11.2 seconds was about average for a 1963 T-Bird with the 300 bhp 390 ci engine.

Problem areas

The Kelsey-Hayes wire wheels may cause punctures if the spokes protrude through the rim and chafe the tube. Flaps are available, or the wheel may be taped. Early wire wheels were known to fail under extreme usage and were recalled.

In 1964 the vacuum system used ¼ inch neoprene lines which can loosen or break. The system was very complicated and was applied to locks, fresh-air vents and heater control valves. The electrical system was also becoming very complex. Owners reported many troubles in these cars even when they were new. Buyers should test all systems.

The steering gear from 1961 to 1964 is the same as that of the Lincoln, and has not had a

The roadster was introduced this year with the fiberglass deck cover and Kelsey-Hayes wire wheels. Genuine knock-off hubs protruded enough to cause removal of the rear fender skirts. The early wire wheels had failures and were recalled. Roadsters lead the Thunderbird market and fine examples are around $20,000.

good service history. Adjustment is not only difficult but sensitive. The cars are prone to wander. Beginning in 1965, the Ford steering gear was used.

Summary and prospects

Auction prices for rather ordinary coupes have been in the $5,000 to $7,000 range with convertibles running as high as $11,000. Pristine examples will bring much more. A 1964 coupe with only 1,500 miles has sold for $20,000. Fine coupes are in the $10,000 to $15,000 range. There were only fifty genuine 1964 roadsters made, which can bring as much as $25,000 to $30,000 per car. Even fake roadsters will go for $15,000 to $20,000.

Appreciation on the 1961-66 cars has been accelerating and prospects are excellent for long-term gains. Good club support has helped. Owners can drive these cars with great pleasure and low operating costs.

Auction prices

1961 T-Bird convertible (2)	$7,000
1962 T-Bird landau (1)	$18,500
1962 T-Bird roadster (2)	$14,800
1963 T-Bird roadster (1)	$25,000
1964 T-Bird coupe (1) 24 K miles	$9,500
1964 T-Bird convertible (2)	$13,250
1965 T-Bird coupe (1)	$11,000

This splendid 1963 T-Bird convertible can approach a price of $20,000 when in best condition. Restoration costs are substantial and average examples can be found at much lower prices.

Production:

	Hardtop	Convertible	Landau	Roadster	Roadster with tri-power***
1961	62,535	10,516	none	none	none
1962	68,127	9,884	none	1,307	120
1963	42,806	5,913	14,139	418	37
1964	60,552	9,198*	22,715	none	none
1965	42,652	6,846	25,474	none	none
1966	13,389	5,049	35,105**	none	none

*includes 40-50 roadsters
**additional blind Landaus in 1966: 15,633
***tri-power = three two-barrel carburetors

The 1964 Thunderbird was restyled and a very handsome car it was. This is the landau model, identified by the mock landau iron on the rear quarter panel. It should bring a slight premium over the coupe. Prices are generally lower than for the 1961-63 series, but the chance for future appreciation remains strong.

A genuine 1964 roadster is very rare and can bring as much as $30,000. Authenticity must be verified as reproduction parts are readily available.

The 1965 Thunderbird was little changed from 1964. Prices for clean coupes will be in the $6,000 to $8,000 range.

The last Thunderbird convertible appeared in 1966—something of a cutoff point for collectors. Convertibles in the 1964-66 series can bring as much as $15,000. The 1967 Thunderbird, with entirely different sheet metal, has much lower value and has not yet drawn substantial collector interest.

Chapter 12

Mustang 1965-1973

★★	Coupe
★★★	Convertible
★★★★	Boss
★★★★★	Shelby

History

The Mustang was introduced on April 17, 1964, and was Ford's most successful product. This spring introduction caused many people to refer to the early Mustangs as 1964½s, but all were considered 1965s by the company.

The new car was based on Falcon compo-

This 1965 Mustang convertible was a calendar prototype. This wonderful design caught the imagination of 110,206 buyers in the first full model year. Convertibles constituted just over 15 percent of production. Today, prices for these open cars in fine shape with the 289 ci solid-lifter 271 bhp engine have broken through to five figures. V-8 engines in lower tune and six-cylinder engines will be worth less. Keep an eye out for the desirable bucket seats and floor-mounted shifters. Remember that the accessory list is extraordinarily large, which will greatly affect value.

nents, but had stunning new proportions. Ford cleverly offered numerous engine options, beginning with a 170 ci Falcon six at 101 bhp. Excitement expanded with the 260 ci V-8 at 164 bhp and the 289 ci engine with four-barrel carbs at 210 bhp.

At the introduction of the regular 1965 line in the fall of 1964, the 289 was offered with two- or four-barrel carbs at 200 and 225 bhp, respectively. The 260 was dropped after only a few months. A 289 with solid lifters and 271 bhp appeared in June 1964. Enthusiasts were dazzled by these power choices.

Various transmissions were offered: a three-speed and a four-speed manual box plus the three-speed C4 Cruise-O-Matic. This transmission was built by Ford until 1981 when it was revised as the C5, with production ending in 1986.

The GT equipment group was offered in April 1965, and included disc brakes, lower-ratio steering (checked by ID tag reading HHC-AW or HHC-AX), the 225 bhp or 271 bhp 289 engine, fog lamps, dual exhausts, five dial instruments and a special handling package of chassis modifications. Many of these items could later be dealer-installed, though collectors like to find factory-original GT packages.

The list of accessories for the Mustang was extraordinary and sellers will usually be quick to point out rare items. Among the more than 130 items were five types of outside mirrors, a tissue dispenser, two types of fire extinguishers, two-way citizens band radio and even a compass.

In the extended 1965 model year, Ford sold 680,989 Mustangs. (*Technically* there were no 1964 Mustangs.) It was record performance for the company.

The Shelby Mustang appeared in 1965, a highly specialized development of the GT theme. Originally the car was in fastback form, but six convertibles were built in 1966. More came in 1968 through 1970.

All Shelbys are exceptionally valuable. In six production years, only 14,368 were produced. For a detailed analysis of this car and market, refer to Peter C. Sessler's *Illustrated High-Performance Mustang Buyer's Guide.*

There was success built upon success for Mustang. For 1966, the 289 engine could be had with Cruise-O-Matic transmission, and

The Mustang fastback, or 2+2, was the third body introduced in 1965, after the initial convertible and notchback coupe. This one had the 289 ci engine. Carroll Shelby used this style for his initial modified Mustangs in 1965. Collectors have given some preference to this style over the original notchback coupe. Prices for average examples will be around $5,000, while superb copies may bring thousands more.

the three-speed unit was dropped from the high-performance engine. The five-dial instrument panel became standard. The Cobra name was used for the top 271 hp 289 ci engine (The symbol for this engine is K.) Options and accessories were even more numerous than in 1965.

The car was subtly restyled in 1967. The big-block 390 4V engine was an option. Again variations and options are myriad. Prospective Mustang buyers should refer to the *Mustang Recognition Guide,* by Dobbs, Farr, Heasley and Kopec, for an exhaustive description of these models.

During 1968, Mustang engine offerings grew complex. Buyers need to know and confirm these various specifications, since values depend in some measure on power. In simplest form they are as follows.

Six-cylinder 200 ci 115 bhp
Six-cylinder 250 ci 155 bhp
289 ci 2V only until midyear
302 ci 4V 230 bhp
302 ci 2V began in 1968
390 ci GT V-8 335 bhp high-performance
427 ci 4V 390 bhp
428 ci Cobra Jet 335 bhp

In 1969, the Mustang was offered in several new high-performance options: the Mach 1, the Boss 429, the Boss 302 and the continuing Shelby. The GT was finished by the end of the year. Buyers who wish to sort out these options should refer to Sessler's *Illustrated High-Performance Mustang Buyer's Guide.*

A luxury Mustang was offered, called the Grande, which had upgraded interior trim, extra sound insulation and additional rubber in the suspension.

Engines were similar to those of 1968, except the 427 was no longer available. A 351 W (Windsor) appeared in 2V and 4V form. The Mach 1 (with the sports-roof flat-backed coupe) offered engines from the 351 to the Cobra Jet 428 Ram Air. The Boss 302 was introduced in March, again as a fastback coupe. There were also about 500 Boss 429s.

For 1970, the line continued. The Windsor

Buyers will no doubt see many of these 1966 coupes since, in all forms and engine options, an incredible 499,751 units were sold. This particular car has the excellent 289 ci engine. Good ones can still be bargains.

351 was joined by the Cleveland 351. It was the last year for the smaller 200 ci six-cylinder, replaced by the 250 ci six which had been an option since 1969.

In 1971, the 429 was discontinued; the horsepower race was abating. The Mustangs remained in production until 1973, finishing up with 250 ci six and the 302 and 351 engines.

Prospective Mustang buyers are pardoned for growing a bit glassy-eyed at this recitation of engines. Mustang enthusiasts are experts in engine specifications, options and accessories, and rarely tire of debate on the minute details of various model specifications.

The average first-time buyer of a nice clean Mustang will usually be offered a basic six-cylinder model or the lowest-tuned V-8, perhaps even with apologies. These cars will give fine performance and long reliability, and they will certainly be bargains when compared to some of the exotics hinted at here. But remember that originality, regardless of model type, remains more important than specification. Even a beat-up high-performance Mustang may cost a great deal, but the shrewd buyer will search for that pristine, low-mileage, perhaps one-owner car which, in the long run, may give the greatest satisfaction.

Identification

1965: Mustang logo with four radiating bars.

1966: Free-standing Mustang logo in grille.

1967: Twin air scoops ahead of rear wheel. Central Mustang logo with four radiating bars in a larger grille opening set flat into front of car. Concave rear panel.

1968: Grille has rectangular mesh behind logo. Rear air scoop very narrow.

1969: Major restyling. Lower with pointed prow. Small Mustang logo on one side.

1970: Small Mustang logo back in center of grille.

1971: Major restyling. Car lower again. Wheelbase increased to 109 inches. Mustang logo more like 1968—set in single, stronger

Minor styling changes marked the 1967 Mustang as enthusiastic buyers continued to flock to the showrooms. This handsome convertible sports the new styled steel wheels and Firestone wide oval tires. Prices are breaking through five figures for good examples.

This 1968 Mustang Shelby GT500 convertible, a tremendous car, is bringing big money, with top prices exceeding $30,000. The 428 ci engine put out 360 bhp. Shelby was able to install a few 427s with 400 bhp using the C6 automatic transmission. The KR (King of the Road) version used the 428 Cobra Jet engine. In this specialized market, thorough research and knowledge is crucial.

G.T.500
GOODYEAR

crossbar.

1972: Script "Mustang" replaced block letters on rear deck.

1973: Mustang logo set against vertical bar backed by rectangular pattern in grille.

The muscle-car variants—the Shelby, Boss, Mach 1 and so on—will have special external markings. Refer to the *Mustang Recognition Guide* for more details.

Performance and utility

With such a variety of specification, Mustang performance is hard to pinpoint. The 1969 Mach 1 with the 428 Cobra Jet engine had 0-60 mph times of under six seconds. A Shelby GT500 could exceed 130 mph. Yet the average six-cylinder 200 ci model would do well to make 60 mph in fifteen seconds.

In any event, the Mustang in all of the standard forms continues to offer reliable and pleasant motoring. Handling is superior to most cars of its era. Maintenance is reasonable and parts are in abundant supply.

Problem areas

Mustang components are rugged, profiting from high production and refinement. Check for the usual rust problems in lower body areas.

Summary and prospects

There are a lot of Mustangs out there. Prices for ordinary models reflect abundance. Among standard models, there is a consistent decline in prices from 1965 to 1973. Prices for superb convertibles may be in the $15,000 and up range for the early cars, descending to around $6,000 for 1973s.

Always remember that extra equipment and accessories will add a lot. V-8 engines are always preferred. Opinion is divided on transmissions, but as power goes up, the four-speed boxes for many become more important. But the C6 automatic is very strong and handles heavy horsepower with ease.

The bottom of the market will be an ordinary and perhaps dirty six-cylinder coupe, which may be found as low as $2,000. Good, average closed Mustangs are bringing prices more like $5,000 today, with convertibles at about a fifty percent premium.

The muscle cars are an entirely different business, with the rare Shelbys command-

This 1968 Fastback GT had the 302 ci engine. Bigger engines were available but few could complain about performance. With appropriate equipment, nice examples of this car can bring $5,000 or more.

ing very strong prices in the $20,000 to $30,000 range. A Shelby convertible is selling for even more. The Boss 429s are much sought after, again with near Shelby-level prices. Boss 302s are next in order of value. Mach 1 prices will be about the same as convertibles of the same year.

Always be on the lookout for the *odd* car. The 1969-73 Grande, the limited-production 1968 California series (and the parallel Colorado high-country special) and the 1967 Pacesetter are examples. There are so many Mustangs that collectors are usually eager to own something different.

Serious Mustang buyers would do well to join one of the clubs and become acquainted with the subtleties of this market. Mustang literature is abundant and rewards study.

No car with such high production in recent times has caught the imagination of so many people. The Mustang is of the perfect vintage for young collectors and has

This 1969 Mustang Sports-Roof had a 390 medallion, but this engine was not common. The fastback style, however, was a big hit and constituted 44.83 percent of production. A good example will be in the $5,000 to $6,000 range. But with the Boss 302 or 429 ci engines, the price will be much higher.

become the entry-level car into the hobby for thousands of enthusiasts.

Ownership of these fine cars is expanding. The future market is assured, pulled upward by the extraordinarily high prices of the muscle cars. The Mustang is one of those wonderful cars that can be driven at very low running cost, with the promise of long-term profit combined with pride of ownership.

Production:

1965	680,989	*1970*	190,727
1966	607,568	*1971*	149,678
1967	472,121	*1972*	125,093
1968	317,404	*1973*	134,867
1969	299,824		

Auction prices

1965 Mustang convertible (1)	$15,000
1965 Mustang convertible GT (1)	$25,000
1965 Mustang convertible (2)	$4,000 L
1965 Mustang coupe (2) 6-cyl	$2,600 L
1966 Mustang convertible 289 (1)	$17,000
1966 Mustang convertible (1)	$9,400
1966 Mustang GT350 hardtop coupe (1)	$9,000
1967 Mustang hardtop (2)	$8,950
1968 Shelby GT500 convertible (2)	$23,000
1968 Mustang GT390 (2)	$8,000
1969 Mustang coupe California Special (2)	$6,500
1969 Mustang Boss 429 (2)	$21,500

The 1969 Mustang Grande featured luxury trim levels, additional sound deadening and a slightly softened ride through the use of special rubber bushings. Production of 22,182 was not small but gives some exclusivity to this special car. Prices could be higher than standard coupes but condition is crucial.

A 1970 Mustang Boss 302 Sports-Roof with 290 bhp. The wheels were odd and did not resemble any of the regular Ford options. Boss-engine Mustangs are always worth a lot more, and this car could bring from $6,000 to $10,000, depending on condition.

The 1970 Mustang Grande had this special roof trim plus other decor improvements. Prices will be below convertibles and the muscle cars.

The 1971 Mustang convertible is a fine collectible which can still be found at reasonable prices. This car sports unusual double-stripe whitewall tires.

This 1972½ Sprint has the USA shield on the rear quarter panel and was offered in red, white and blue color combinations. The model may have been inspired by the Olympics. The big 429 engine was gone and power was down in the remaining detuned engines.

The last Mustang convertible was in 1973, and it would be the final Ford convertible of the seventies. 11,853 were sold. As a "last" car, it had some notoriety. Prices for these final convertibles are around $5,000, with fine examples bringing perhaps $7,000.

Chapter 13

Torino 1968-1971

★

History

The Torino began in 1968 as an upgraded Fairlane. The six-cylinder 250 ci engine was standard. The 289 ci engine was offered in the GT with the 302 and 390 engines optional. Convertibles were offered from

This 1968 Torino was the first year of production, and a superb convertible might make $6,000 or $7,000. Prices decline in subsequent years.

the beginning.

In 1969, the Torino took on a fresh, independent nameplate identity. The 302 engine became standard; the 351 W (Windsor) and the 390 were optional. The 428 CJ was at the top of the power choices. In 1970 the 390 was dropped and the 429 replaced the 428. Also, the 351 C (Cleveland) made its debut alongside the 351 W. The Torino prospered as the decade closed but the convertibles were phased out in 1971.

Identification

The Torino shared basic Fairlane specifications. The GT used the 116 inch long wheelbase. "Torino" and "Grand Touring" nameplates are found on this series. The NASCAR racing Talladega of 1969 has a flush-fitting grille and more frontal streamlining.

Utility and performance

The Torinos were colossal performers. The 1969 Torino GT Sports Roof with the Cobra Jet 428 engine had a 0-60 mph time of just over six seconds. The big engines provided exceptional power-to-weight ratios, but the car was nose-heavy with lots of understeer. But one could hardly fault the power of the 390 or even the 302. Torinos really move!

The Torino Talladega Sports-Roof of 1969 was a NASCAR competition car beginning with the 427 engine, used only because the 429 was not yet homologated. The general public received a 428 Cobra Jet engine.

Performance cost money. Gasoline mileage was fair, and these big-engine Torinos and full-size Fords might achieve 14 mpg under optimum driving conditions. But premium gasoline was cheap.

This 1970 Torino GT hardtop had the 302 ci engine. If it were fitted with either the 351 or 429 ci engine, there would be a plaque on the side of the front fender. It had Magnum 500 wheels. Nice examples of this car can bring $2,500 and up.

The 1971 Torino two-door Brougham is a good solid car but collectors have not yet sought these closed bodies. Many are still being junked and good examples can be found at very low prices.

1971

The Torino model appeared in 1968 and has achieved collectible status by virtue of convertibles offered through 1971. These convertibles are not expensive and make fine entry-level cars for enthusiasts. This 1970 model with the 351 ci engine can be bought in average condition for about $3,500, with superior examples for $5,000 or more. Keep a lookout for the 429 ci engine option and four-speed transmission.

Problem areas

Buyers of these relatively recent Fords have the benefit of substantial junkyard parts availability. But the cars were tough and strong and, unless they have been greatly abused, are likely to be very long-lived. Rust may be a problem, but production was strong and there are many good cars to choose from.

Summary and prospects

The Torino has only recently found collector interest, and the convertible and GT hardtops are presently being sought. The big-engine cars have the greatest appeal because they are the last of the muscle cars. Convertibles in fine shape are now in the $5,000 and up range, with the hardtops somewhat lower.

Cobra Jet-engined Torinos should be rated at least two stars. Condition will be very important because few collectors have undertaken serious restorations, as the cars do not yet have enough value to justify heavy investment. This will cause junking to continue, and the market in the near future will remain fairly soft.

But as the abundant supply of Torinos gradually shrinks, the appreciation should be slow and steady. Here is another car for entry-level collectors who can enjoy depreciation-free motoring in the grand style.

Production (convertible GT):

1968 5,310
1969 2,552
1970 3,939
1971 1,613

Auction prices

1970 Torino Cobra Jet coupe (2)	$7,400
1970 Torino GT convertible (2)	$4,000
1971 Torino GT convertible (2)	$5,100

Appendix

Engines and high performance

There are at least seventy-five different engine specifications for post-1945 Fords, and buyers may well be confused when confronting seller's claims. The problem is further complicated by the visual similarity of several engine types and the reuse of engine code numbers for different engines in different years.

Nevertheless, an understanding of the many different types of Ford engines will be useful in appraising a Ford collectible. Since performance is crucial in the sixties, knowledge of the principal performance options is also important since car value may hinge on claims of sellers about engine specifications.

Buyers usually familiarize themselves with the engine codes on the data or patent plate. The vehicle identification number, or VIN, is discussed later. The engine letter is first in the serial numbers through 1959 and fifth beginning in 1960.

In addition, when exceptional claims are made by the seller, a check on engine casting numbers is useful. Even then, parts can be swapped, such as the obvious valve cover and manifolds or even the more subtle components such as heads. A 352 engine can readily masquerade as a mighty 427 engine.

There are eight primary engines types in the period under review which follow this system. In all cases on the list below, the three numbers are for cubic inch displacement (ci) unless followed by bhp. All engines are overhead valve unless otherwise specified. And V means venturi and refers to the number of barrels in the carburetor.

Six-cylinder engines

Ford six-cylinder engines began in 1941 with the G series L-head having a 226 ci displacement. An ohv six (Engine code A) appeared in 1952 with 215 ci displacement, bored out to 223 ci in 1954. Brake horsepower ranged from 115 to 145. This engine remained essentially unchanged until 1964. The small Falcon six was added to the range in 1960 with 144 ci and was stroked to 170 ci in 1962 for use in the Fairlane and enlarged again to 200 ci in 1964. Buyers of six-cylinder cars are usually not interested in performance.

226 G (GA) L-head 1941-47
H (HA) 1947-51
215 A ohv 1952 and 1953
223 A 1954-59
V 1960-64
144 S 1960-64 (in Falcons) 90 bhp
170 U 1962 forward
200 T 1964 forward
240 V 1965-70
E taxi 150 bhp,
B police (there is a truck B engine with 300 ci and 170 bhp)

L-head V-8

The early period from 1946 to 1953 is straightforward. The 1939 239 ci 95 bhp flathead Mercury V-8 engine was fitted to the 1946 Fords with a 100 bhp rating. There were changes in head design and ignition placement for the 1949 model along with other minor improvements. The general serial letter designation for L-head engines is A. This engine was also used in the 1946-48 Mercuries and was stroked in 1949 for Mercury use with a displacement of 255 ci. In this stroked form it was also used as a police (P) engine. Production ended with the 1953 model.

Y-block

In 1954 the Y-block ohv V-8 engine was introduced, so called because of its cross-section appearance.

Ford used the following code system for engine numbers on the Y-block.

239 U 1954
272 U 1955
272 B 1957
272 M 1955
292 P 1955
312 P 1956
312 D 1957
312 F 1957 300 bhp supercharged, Thunderbird
312 E 1957 270 bhp hi-performance, 285 bhp racing
292 C 1958

The 312 engine is the preferred engine in this series though it has only modest influence when weighted against general car condition. The rare F-series brings very high prices in Thunderbirds.

FE series

In 1958, Ford introduced the big-block FE series engine with an initial 332 ci displacement. This engine proliferated into more than twenty-three variants ranging up to the mighty 427 ci job with 425 hp, first offered in 1963, and the 428 first offered in 1966. Since engine size and power affect value in the sixties cars, buyers need to confirm what is being offered, especially since casual exterior identification may not help, especially with these big-block engines.

332 B 2V 1958-59
G 4V 1958

352 H 4V 1958-59 identical to 332 ci mechanically apart from stroke size, increase 0.2 inch
X 2V 1960-63, 1967-70
X 4V 1964-66
Y 4V 1960

390 Z 4V 1961-68 300 bhp
Z 4V 1961 only 375 bhp
Z 6V 1961 400 bhp. Note that the same engine code is used on three variations which can be confusing to both buyer and seller
P 4V 1962-66 police
R 4V 1961-62 export
Q 4V 1962 special
Y 2V 1966-71
H 2V 1964-68
X 2V 1967-69 premium fuel
S 4V 1966-69 GT (390 continued until 1971 with other codes; also used in trucks until 1976)

406 B 4V 1962-63
G 6V 1962-63 racing engine with many modifications. A very few may have the desirable cross-bolt main bearings after mid-1962

427 Q 4V 1963-64 410 bhp
R 8V 1963-67 425 bhp
M 8V 1965-67 sohc
L 4V 1965-67 sohc both available only from Ford dealers over-the-counter and not fitted in production
W 4V 1966-68 hi-performance

428 Q 4V 1966-70 an enlarged 390
P 4V 1967-70 police
R-4V 1968-70 Cobra Jet with Ram Air

As the horsepower race abated, the big-block engine was phased out and last appeared in 1971.

427

The mighty 427 engine was the most powerful standard car engine offered by Ford. It was offered only with a four-speed box. Normal carburetion was two four-venturis with dual cut-in feature. A high-rise manifold was available for better flow. Exhaust valves were made of 21-4N forged steel with chrome-plated stems and hard sili chrome tips. Like the smaller engines, the face and seating of intake valves were aluminized. The combustion chamber was wedge shaped. Solid valve lifters were fitted. In 1963 and 1964 the pistons were similar to those of the 289 with the raised pads on the faces to contact the valve face when necessary under extreme conditions.

An important feature are the cross-bolted main bearing caps which reinforce bearing alignment and provide increased rigidity of the crankcase. The bolt heads are clearly visible just above the pan joint. The 427 also offered an oil relief valve to prevent excessive pressure during cold starts. The big 11½ inch clutch was noncentrifugal, unlike that of the smaller engines.

An expensive transistorized ignition was an early option on the 1964 427 but was not too popular. Axle ratios used with the 427 were 3.5 and 4.11:1, a tribute to the extraordinary revving ability of this massive engine.

The "side oiler" blocks with oil galleries to the left of the main are considered the best engine for top performance and were the basis for the ohc models. Production began on March 1, 1965.

The heads of the cross-bolt mains on 406s and 427s are easily seen above the oil pan joint in the block. This layout includes main bearing caps and spacers in a matched set which must be present in the block.

This great 427 engine was rated at 425 bhp at 6000 rpm with 480 lb-ft of torque at 3700 rpm. The compression was very high at 11.1:1. It represents the pinnacle of sheer power in Ford engine development. Though these engines are not in short supply, be careful when one is offered in any car because the visual differences between the 427 and lesser engines are often not apparent. Decals and chrome may mislead.

428

The 428 was introduced in 1966, a 406 engine with a long-stroke crank from the 410 Mercury. It resembles the 390 in specification. It was designed to provide high, continuous and lazy power. It was the right engine for the big Galaxies and LTDs where it was called the 7 Liter. Even the Police Interceptor model had hydraulic valve lifters after 1966.

In 1968 the Cobra Jet version appeared with Ram Air; the Super CJ engine followed with external oil and other goodies. These two engines established the 428 as much more than a limousine hauler.

The 428 remained in production through 1970.

90-degree V-8 series

In 1962 the new small-block V-8 engine was introduced, more compact and lighter than the Y-block. There are two basic periods, defined by bell housing configurations, namely five-bolt through 1964, and six-bolt thereafter. Interchangeability of blocks is determined largely by the bell housing. For Ford use, it was built in seven basic sizes:

221 L 2V 1962-63
260 F 2V 1962-64
289 C 2V 1963-68
A 4V 1963-68 premium fuel
289HP K 4V 1962-67 high performance with mechanical lifters, heavy main bearing caps, orange paint at rear
302 F 2V 1968-72
D 2V 1969-72 taxi or police
J 4V 1968 premium fuel
302 Boss G 1969-70 Boss engine with modifications, four-bolt mains, thick walls, large valves. Early Boss 302 engines in 1969 had a problem with cracked pistons which was corrected in production
351 W (Windsor) H 2V 1969-72 used mostly in big Fords
M 4V 1969 only "performance" year

This 1962 V-8 engine has continued in production and, as downsizing occurred in the industry, has turned out to be the "big" V-8 engine of the eighties.

385 series

A clean-burning antismog big engine was needed as the sixties drew to a close to replace the 390, 427 and 428. The 385 series was very tough and, as the 429, turned out to be a splendid performance unit. It was built in two sizes.

429 N 4V 1968-72 Thunderbird
K 2V 1969-71 Ford

429CJ C 4V Cobra Jet 4V 1970-71 hydraulic cams, (1971 4-bolt mains)
J as above with Ram Air 1970 (Torino), 1971

429 SCJ Super Cobra Jet 4V 4-bolt main bearing caps, mechanical lifters

429 Boss Z 4V 1969-70 Mustang all-out high-performance engine, street version engine tag 820-T

429S Boss NASCAR engine, engine tag 820-S

460 A 4V 1968 forward. Initially a Lincoln engine but fitted to Ford and Thunderbirds in 1973

429

The 429, last of the "big three," was introduced in 1968 as a replacement for both the 427 and the 428. It had a short stroke of 3.59 inches with a big 4.36 inch bore. This engine used thin-wall casting techniques with an iron head with wedge-shaped combustion chambers.

The Boss 429 engine was exceptional in many ways. It was really a hemi-head engine but was called a "crescent head" to avoid conflict with Chrysler. Aluminum heads used O-rings instead of gaskets. Four-bolt main bearing caps were used, extending into the webs to stabilize the mains. The 429S was intended as a NASCAR competition engine and though listed as an option, it was never promoted by Ford because the company could not sell it for a profit. It was homologated in the 1969 and 1970 Mustang.

It had a short life and became redundant by the close of competition activities at Ford. Production of the Boss 429 ceased in mid-1970.

These great 429s, especially in these powerful specifications, add substantially to the value of any car. Collectors seem to pay the most for the Boss 429 engine which was accompanied by the huge hood scoop, and decals on the Mustang. The 429 Cobra Jet would be the next most sought after engine.

335 series

A clean-burning antismog engine was needed between the 302 and the 390 and especially to replace the aging 352 FE unit. The 351 Cleveland unit, introduced in 1970, had up-to-date engineering such as the canted-valve cylinder head design, superior to the 351 Windsor. It was a tough unit and remained in production into the eighties. The 351 was used most often in the Mustang and Torino. Note that the H and M engine codes parallel Windsor production. Also note that bhp figures dropped rapidly after 1970.

351 C H 2V begin 1970 (250 bhp, dropping to 177 bhp by 1972)

351 C M 4V 1970-74

351 Boss R 4V 1971 only (330 bhp)

351 HO R 4V (High Output) 1971-72 275 bhp, a detuned 351 Boss

351 CJ Q 4V 1972-73 266 bhp

400 S 2V 1971-78

MEL

The 430 was used in the 1959 and 1960 Thunderbird but was primarily fitted to the Mercury, Edsel and Lincoln in various sizes. This is a heavy engine which was introduced in 1958 in the Lincoln. The added performance and rarity makes the 430 more desirable for collectors even though handling is slightly degraded. The standard Thunderbird 352 FE engine was new in 1958 and parts are more readily available. The 390 FE is sometimes fitted to the Thunderbird by collectors as it is virtually indistinguishable from the 352.

Other engines

Ford built larger V-8 truck engines such as the 477 and 534 which are low revving and have very high torque. These engines are unrelated to any of the above series. Once in a great while an imaginative owner may install one of these commercial units in a car but the resulting novelty has little utility.

Patent plates and serial numbers

Ford products have an identifying metal tag which can provide information on the original specification of the car. This tag or patent plate is mounted in various locations:

- 1949 on dash panel under hood
- 1950 (as of April 1) front face or top of cowl panel under hood
- 1951 (as of May 23) upper right-hand side of dash panel by engine
- 1952 right front body pillar below hinge opening
- 1953-54 mounted on left front body pillar
- 1955-56 left front body pillar except Thunderbird where plate is on dash panel in engine compartment
- 1957 and afterward left front door body pillar or lock face

When reading a 1950-52 data plate, the following alpha-numeric system is used as a serial number:

- 1st digit, engine: B = V-8 239 ci
  H = 6-cyl 225 ci
  A = 6-cyl ohv 215 ci
  P = Police 355 ci V-8
- 2nd digit, year: 0 = 1950, 1 = 1951, 2 = 1952
- 3rd & 4th digits, assembly plant: AT = Atlanta, BF = Buffalo, CS = Chester, CH = Chicago, DL = Dallas, DA = Dearborn, EG = Edgewater, KC = Kansas City, LB = Long Beach, LU = Louisville, MP = Memphis, NR = Norfolk, RH = Richmond, SR = Somerville, SP = St. Paul, HM = Highland Park
- 5th to 10th digits, production numbers

When reading a 1953-59 data plate, the following alpha-numeric system is used as a serial number:

- 1st digit, engine type
- 2nd digit, year: 4 = 1954, 5 = 1955, etc.
- 3rd digit, assembly plant: A = Atlanta, B = Buffalo, C = Chester, G = Chicago, D = Dallas, F = Dearborn, E = Edgewater or Mahwah, H = Highland Park, K = Kansas City, L = Long Beach, L = Lorain (after 1953), U = Louisville, M = Memphis, N = Norfolk, R = Richmond or San Jose, S = Somerville, P = St Paul/Twin Cities
- 4th digit, body type
- 5th to 10th digits, production numbers

When reading a 1960 and later data plate, the following alpha-numeric system is used in the box entitled "serial number," "vehicle warranty number" or "vehicle identification number":

- 1st digit, year: 0 = 1960, 1 = 1961, and repeats at 1970
- 2nd digit, assembly plant: A = Atlanta, B = Oakville, Canada, D = Dallas, E = Mahwah, F = Dearborn, G = Chicago, H = Lorain, J = Los Angeles, K = Kansas City, N = Norfolk, P = St. Paul/Twin Cities, R = San Jose, S = Pilot Plant, T = Metuchen, U = Louisville, W = Wayne, X = St. Thomas, Y = Wixom, Z = St Louis
- 3rd and 4th digits, series and body style
- 5th digit, engine
- 6th to 11th digits, production numbers

For 1946-49 information, see Chapters 1 and 2.

PATENT PLATE DIAGRAM

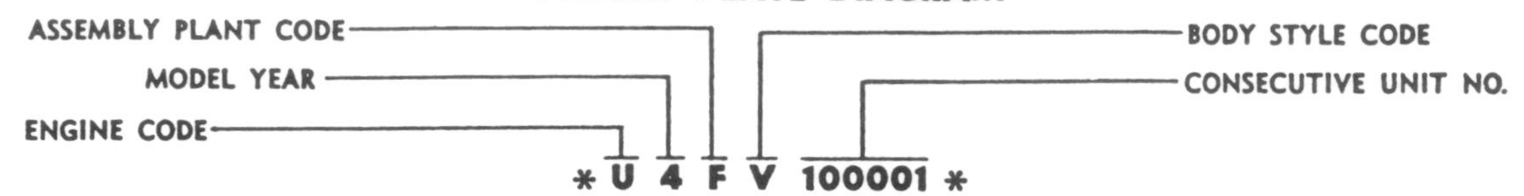

The asterisks before and after the complete serial number are inserted to assure that no other digits or letters can be added to the Serial Number.

Serial Number (*U4FV100001*)
"U" – 8 Cyl. OHV Engine – 239 Cu. in. displacement
"4" – 1954 Model
"F" – Assembled at Dearborn Plant
"V" – Victoria body style
"100001" – First Car Assembled

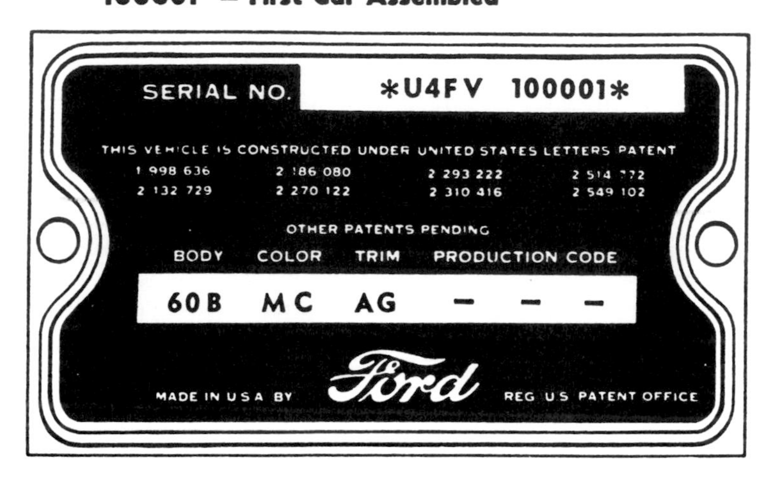

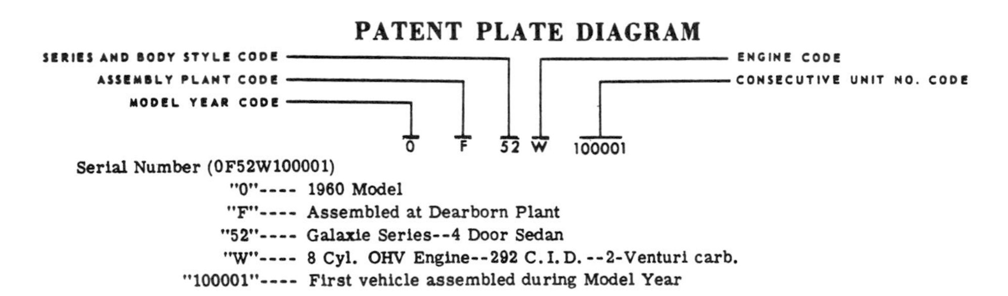

Serial Number (0F52W100001)
"0"---- 1960 Model
"F"---- Assembled at Dearborn Plant
"52"---- Galaxie Series--4 Door Sedan
"W"---- 8 Cyl. OHV Engine--292 C.I.D.--2-Venturi carb.
"100001"---- First vehicle assembled during Model Year

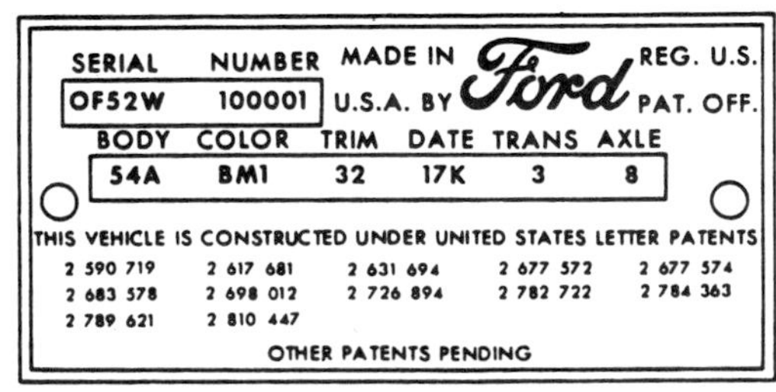

1960 - 61 P-3154

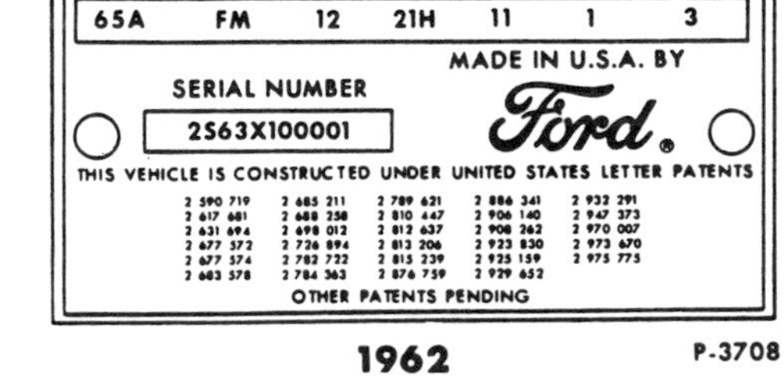

1962 P-3708

Four-speed transmission

A four-speed manual transmission was manufactured by Ford Transmission and Controls Division. It is identified by a top cover with ten bolts. This transmission was brought out in 1964 and was used until 1973. Two sets of gear ratios were offered.

Gear	Standard	Close-ratio
1st	2.78:1	2.32:1
2nd	1.93:1	1.69:1
3rd	1.36:1	1.29:1
4th	1:1	1:1

Generally speaking, the 260 V-8 used the close-ratio four-speed if the car had 3.50 or lower speed gear ratio (that is, higher numerically such as the 4.11). If the axle ratio was 3.25 or higher speed (lower numerically such as 3.0), then the wide-ratio transmission was fitted because of the need for a lower first gear.

The four-speed transmission behind the 428 engines used a large input shaft.

A Borg-Warner four-speed transmission was used in the 1961-63 Galaxie, the 1963-65 Fairlane and Falcon, and the 1965-66 Mustang. This transmission is not nearly as strong as the Ford Transmission and Controls four-speed.

Another four-speed transmission was offered for the Falcon and Mustang six-cylinder and was built in Dagenham, England. It was suitable for light duty. The ratios were:

1st 3.162:1
2nd 2.214:1
3rd 1.412:1
4th 1:1

Clubs

Fabulous Fifties Ford Club of America
PO Box 286
Riverside, CA 92502

Ford Galaxie Club of America
1014 Chestnut St PO Box 2206
Bremerton, WA 98310

Classic Thunderbird Club International
PO Box 4148
Santa Fe Springs, CA 90670-1148

Fairlane Club of America
819 Milwaukee Ave
Denver, CO 80206

Crown Victoria Association
Rt 5
Bryan, OH 43506

International Ford Retractable Club
PO Box 92
Jerseyville, IL 62052

Special Interest Fords of the 50's
23018 Berry Pine Dr
Spring, TX 77373

The Falcon Club of America
629 N Hospital Dr
Jacksonville, AZ 72076

1954 Ford Club of America
2314 Wakeforest Ct
Arlington, TX 76012

The Mustang Club of America
PO Box 447
Livonia, GA 30058

Mustang Owner's Club
2829 Cagua Dr NE
Albuquerque, NM 87110

'71 429 Mustang Registry
PO Box 1472
Fair Oaks, CA 95628

Nifty Fifties Ford Club
PO Box 142
Macedonia, OH 44056

Vintage T Bird Club of America
PO Box 23250
Dearborn, MI 48123

Thunderbirds of America
PO Box 2766
Cedar Rapids, IA 52406

Mustang and Classic Ford Club
PO Box 963
North Attleboro, MA 02761

Associated Fords of the 50s
PO Box 66161
Portland, OR 97226

Performance Ford Club of America
PO Box 32
Asheville, OH 43103

Suggested reading list

There are over eighty titles in print on post-war Fords, more than half of which are on the Mustang. In addition there are many technical and shop manuals plus racing and high-performance books and catalogs.

Illustrated High-Performance Mustang Buyer's Guide by Peter Sessler, Motorbooks International, 1983. Detailed information on some very valuable and esoteric Mustangs.

The Nifty Fifties Ford by Ray Miller and Glenn Embree, Evergreen Press, 1974. A lavish photographic essay with helpful text.

Mustang Recognition Guide by Larry Dobbs, et al., Dobbs Publications, 1981. Excellent detailed specification and pictures.

Big Fords and Mercs. A Source Book 1957 thru 1970 by Samuel A. Shields, Jr., Motorbooks International, 1984. Brief statements with reprinting of original literature.

Classic Motorbooks Ford Retractable Photofacts by Jerry H. Magayne, Motorbooks International, 1983. Excellent coverage of the retractable.

The Mustangs 1964-1973 by Richard Langworth, Motor Racing Publications, 1984. General introduction with many pictures.

Thunderbird, An Odyssey in Automotive Design by William P. Boyer, Taylor Publishing Company, 1986. A handsome history of the Thunderbird with much color. Reprint in color of sales literature.

Fearsome Fords 1959-1973 by Phil Hall, Motorbooks International, 1982. Fine study of high-performance models.